Additional Praise for
Happier at Work

"I highly recommend this book! *Happier at Work* is an essential and timely guide brimming with insights, a depth of experience and backed up by science. You can achieve a healthier and happier workforce! Gayle Van Gils illuminates the path."

—ELISHA GOLDSTEIN, PHD
Author of *Uncovering Happiness*

"Thousands of us show up a work each day looking for happiness and too often we are left unfulfilled. But maybe what we are searching for is closer than we think. If you want to awaken the transformative power of love, wisdom and mindfulness in your daily work, read this book."

—MICHAEL CARROLL
Author of *"Awake at Work"* and *"The Mindful Leader"*

"In *Happier at Work,* Gayle Van Gils uses a lifetime of experience teaching mindfulness and leadership training to deliver crucial tools to the workplace. Beyond just teaching mindfulness as a path to stress relief, her ideas show us how to be the sort of person who enjoys each day that confident and loving colleague that coworkers actually want to be around."

—ETHAN NICHTERN
Author of *The Road Home*

Happier at Work

Happier
at Work

The Power of Love
to Transform the Workplace

Gayle Van Gils

SHE WRITES PRESS

Published 2017
Printed in the United States of America
Print ISBN: 978-1-63152-204-8
E-ISBN: 978-1-63152-205-5
Library of Congress Control Number: 2017932872

For information, address:
She Writes Press
1563 Solano Ave #546
Berkeley, CA 94707

Cover design © Julie Metz, Ltd./metzdesign.com
Interior design by Tabitha Lahr

She Writes Press is a division of SparkPoint Studio, LLC.

Names and identifying characteristics have been changed to protect the privacy of certain individuals.

This book is dedicated to all people who work, in hopes that your lives will be filled with love and inspiration.

Contents

Chapter 3: Transform the Energy of Fear

Chapter 4: Listen and Be Heard

Chapter 5: Be Kind to Yourself

Chapter 6: Connect and Succeed

Chapter 7: Radiate Confidence

Chapter 8: Engage and Thrive

Appendix A: Table of Exercises
and Practices

What's Love Got To Do With It?

"What you think is what you get" is a popular saying. This becomes a real challenge in a world where negative news and opinions are broadcast nonstop. If we absorb this negativity, we can become judgmental and fearful of others, and self-critical to the point of insecurity—all of which profoundly affects how we live our lives.

Our workplaces are a clear reflection of the beliefs of our times, and of a social system in which fear and suspicion of others too often trumps knowledge and compassion. This cultural climate of negativity, fear, divisiveness, and self-interest has created a lot of pain for a lot of people. While I don't have all the answers, I wrote this book to address this workplace pain openly and directly, with the intention of sharing practices and attitudes that will positively impact lives at work on a daily basis. It is possible to shift your current situation and discover how open hearts and minds can create workplaces full of engagement, community, collaboration, creativity, and joy.

With the formal and informal practices of mindfulness offered here, you can start to relate to your work, colleagues, clients, and customers in a totally new way. The practice of mindfulness will not only improve your cognitive performance, reduce your stress, and ventilate your hectic day; it will also lead to increased openness, curiosity, empathy, and engagement. These enhanced benefits derive from the opening of heart and mind that mindfulness initiates—an opening that's increased by practices of compassion that can be naturally and easily integrated into your workday. These small, incremental habits will have huge benefits for you personally, and for your workplace as well.

For as long as I can remember, I have been inspired to find and accentuate the good, the potential, and the best in being human. However, my first experiences in a corporate environment were not particularly supportive of this approach. After earning an MBA at UCLA, I entered the workforce at a managerial level and immediately experienced difficulties being accepted. There were jealousies from internal candidates who did not get the position I had been awarded. This aroused territorial instincts that resulted in people withholding information from me and watching me to catch any mistakes I might make. Generally, few moments of human goodness were extended to me. I did my best to forge relationships with my colleagues and lead my team, but I did not yet have the skills to understand what was happening, and I had not yet recognized how I might be an agent of change regarding the negative dynamic I found myself in.

Discouraged, I left that position after a year. Now, years later, after having worked with many individuals in many workplaces, I understand what skills are needed to undo negative behaviors at work—and I know that they are both teachable and easily accessible to everyone who wishes to implement them.

The positive experience of goodness in life is connected with opening our hearts and tearing down the walls that separate us from each other and keep us from being intimately in touch with our world. It takes a lot of courage to open our hearts to ourselves in the workplace—a place that may not feel safe due to current norms of behavior. Yet opening is exactly the answer to the constriction that cuts off communication and collaboration in an unhealthy work environment. When you courageously open yourself to and touch the hidden treasure of goodness within your own being, you experience it viscerally—you feel it in your chest. You might recognize it when you feel vulnerable, exposed, and tentative. What you are touching is compassion, or love, an emotion we all know and need and yet has for too long been excluded from the realm of work. When you open yourself to feel, you also open the door for others to feel and communicate with you.

Why Love?

Love is an expansive emotion. It opens us up. When your behavior is inspired by the emotion of love and connection rather than the fear and constriction that often dominates at work, your opened state of mind is more curious, creative, collaborative, and compassionate. An open mind is interested, has the patience to listen and understand and consider other points of view. When our minds open to truly take in more than our own position and desires, there exists an expanded possibility of shifting the culture of our workplaces away from a narrow and egotistical orientation. We reap an outpouring and sharing of ideas and innovation when we no longer feel shut down or afraid to share our talents. The spirit-killing activities of constant judgment, intolerance of failure, and over-control are holdovers from a different era of business. Those methods may have seemed practical in a factory environment, but they were certainly never inspiring.

Today's workplaces can only thrive if we discover and implement strategies that reduce and manage stress and encourage flexible thinking and open communication, allowing our businesses to prosper in these times of uncertainty, global competition, resource depletion, and an ever-growing knowledge economy. Companies such as Aetna, Goldman Sachs, BlackRock, General Mills, Green Mountain Coffee, SAP, and others have implemented mindfulness programs, and as a result they're experiencing a happier and healthier workforce that is more focused, less stressed, and more productive. The ways in which mindfulness and love as compassionate engagement can work to improve our lives and livelihood is the next frontier in business practice. Love is the emotion that opens our hearts and connects us to each other and to the greater good, and it's what is needed to cure the dysfunctions of the modern workplace.

First Encounters with Compassion

I discovered the journey described in this book when I was eighteen and I enrolled in a class at Smith College called "Mahayana Buddhism," taught by a visiting Zen monk. Our final exam consisted of a single question presented in a private interview with the teacher: "Why did the Buddha teach after he became enlightened?"

We hadn't specifically discussed this in class, so I hesitated as I considered. Finally, I answered, "The Buddha taught because of compassion."

The monk's face lit up with joy. "You understand, you really do!" he said. "Now you need to begin practicing meditation."

At the time, I took his excitement as praise for answering the question correctly. It would take another five years before I followed his advice and began a meditation practice. Once I did, I enjoyed the calm and clarity that arose from my practice, but in the beginning I still did not make the connection between the meditation technique of following my breath and the response I had given to the monk's question. The simple practice of sitting initially helped me deal with frustration and emotional melt-downs resulting from the disappointments of life, but as time went on, it led to shifts in me. They were small and incremental, but also life-changing. I was opening up to compassion.

I moved forward in my life—starting a career, getting married, having a family. When my kids were three and seven, my older son, Alex, started campaigning for a dog. As a result of practicing years of meditation, I thought before responding. Upon doing so, I realized I was telling myself a familiar story about being too busy, not needing more responsibility, and other reasons why I did not want to have a pet in the family—and I had an "aha" moment. I recognized that saying no to having a pet was one of the ways in which I had been closing my heart to a part of life.

Kelsy was a beautiful, red-haired mutt who had to find a home or face the prospect of euthanasia. My friend who had been caring for Kelsy but could no longer keep her invited me to take a walk with them. When we met, my heart opened wide and I found space to love beyond my self-imposed boundary. I was able to shift from my "me first" attitude, and my kids were thrilled by my change of heart.

It is of course possible that my heart might have opened to Kelsy without a meditation practice. However, in going through this experience I recognized a connection between noticing (rather than believing) my egocentric stories and this sudden change of heart. I felt a simple and natural expanding of my comfort zone to include more of the world, and Kelsy was a representation of that expansion.

It is this very unfolding of greater empathy and care that can help us venture beyond our current limitations at work. At work, we all have our stories about our areas of responsibility, our domains of expertise, what we are not interested in, and our fixed beliefs about the way things should be done. If we can see our own stories—one of the benefits of a mindfulness practice—they no longer need to limit us. Opening both our minds and our hearts at work allows an incredible wealth of creativity, optimism, shared vision, and talent to transform our workplaces. This opening of our heart and connecting with our innate compassion surpasses the perks of stress reduction and emotional well-being that accrue from mindfulness practice alone; this practice also begins to affect our relationships, motivation, and leadership style in ways that profoundly help our world.

Mindfulness as a Key to Unlock the Heart

According to countless reports and articles, today's workers experience longer hours, constant input and interruption, and higher expectations of output, all with little personal care and support from management. The mind is often on information overload, and individuals are frequently told to "leave their feelings at the door." Overwhelm has reached a critical point, and attention to work is suffering as a result.

Mindfulness meditation is an antidote to this reality. When you first begin a mindfulness or meditation practice, you are learning to train your faculty of attention, develop ease and relaxation within your mind and body, and experience some peace and space from your noisy mind. As you become calmer and more centered, you perceive clearly what is happening in ever-widening awareness. This includes an awareness of the anxiety, frustration, and sadness, as well as the positive emotions, of others. What I understand now, and perhaps with "beginner's mind" realized when I answered my professor's question all those years ago, is that we are all inextricably interconnected. The awareness and joy that accompanied the Buddha's enlightenment, and any measure of individual awakening, also illuminates the suffering and discontent that others are experiencing. That awareness of the pain of others is why he taught. With expanding awareness, our awakened heart can open to include and soothe others, so we are no longer holding on to pleasure only for ourselves.

When the Buddha experienced his "awakening," he woke up to the innate goodness that was his—and everyone else's—nature. He saw that resistance to life, rather than accepting it as it unfolds moment by moment, is what induces stress and anxiety. He felt compelled to share this good news with others and let them know that they too could become reconnected to each moment, their lives, and their core purpose as human beings.

In the past decade, meditation—also known as mindfulness practice—has become more accepted as a life tool to develop attention and focus, both in personal life and in a growing number of corporate environments. Meditation has been scientifically proven to develop new neural pathways, help us develop new, healthier habits, relieve stress, and increase happiness. We all have access to this ancient (yet thoroughly modern) wisdom. I am inspired to share how mindfulness is also the key to unlocking and opening the heart, a process that can profoundly transform each of our lives and the culture of business as we know it.

With a growing openness to mindfulness practice and its potential benefits for individual and corporate well-being and resilience, these practices can support individuals who wish to be leaders in improving the quality of life, collaboration, team dynamics, communication, and productivity in their own place of work. This book illustrates how patterns of interaction such as inattentive listening, judgmental criticism, lack of empathy, and constant distraction—patterns that cause stress, illness, and disengagement—can be recognized as temporary rather than fundamental, and how confusion, not our basic nature, is what causes these imbalances. By reconnecting with the truth of our goodness, and that of others, we can dispel the confusion, heal our workplaces, and thrive together.

My Journey

My personal journey of growth in learning and applying mindfulness and compassion has included in-depth study and experience on several fronts. In the world of meditation, I was an early student of the great Tibetan Buddhist meditation master Chogyam Trungpa, and I now study under his son, Sakyong Mipham. I am a senior teacher, a Shastri, in the Shambhala Buddhist lineage, and have worked with thousands of students over the years. After receiving my MBA in 1983, I began a career that has included corporate training, executive coaching, and strategic planning. I have taught the connection between contemplative practice and leadership in several coaching and leadership programs. I was also an executive at a technology startup that created a space on the web to assist individuals attempting the intentional change discussed in this book. I've had the opportunity to connect groups of international change leaders on numerous occasions, both as a recurring presenter at Deepak Chopra's "Alliance for a New Humanity" and as an invited delegate to the Dalai Lama's "Connecting for Change" initiative, which brought together Nobel laureates, change leaders, and philanthropists.

Over the years, as a life coach, business coach, and meditation mentor, I have heard the personal stories of frustration, limitation, and dread that individuals associate with their daily work. When I lead programs combining the practices of mindfulness and compassion with everyday life and business life, I offer personal interviews and small discussion circles where participants can openly share their concerns. I have found that after weekend meditation seminars, the participants' main fear is that they will have to shut back down their tender hearts when they walk into their workplace on Monday. Some have even openly cried in frustration at the prospect.

Of course, not every workplace is this dire, and I cover in this book some of the wonderful leaders and organizations that have succeeded by implementing love and compassion in their cultural mix. But let's face it: those of us supported each day to do our best at work are the lucky ones. I would like to increase the odds that everyone who wishes to can be part of changing the culture of their personal and business interactions—that each of us who wishes to can seed a movement to transform the culture of our work and our world.

If we are to create a world in which we wish to live, work, and thrive, we have to engage in investigation, reflection, and honesty. The good news is that our suffering, fears, and habits can be changed through a confluence of the worlds of psychology, neuroscience, and contemplative traditions. In the pages that follow, I will weave these strands together to show how they can refashion the culture of leadership and work in positive and exciting ways.

CHAPTER 1:

You Are the Key to Change

There is so much that is currently not functioning well in our companies. Some of these issues will be personally imperative for you to address if you want to change your experience at work and the culture of your workplace. In this chapter we will first look at some of the problems you may be facing, and then examine a path toward solving them. Tackling these issues head-on is no small feat, and yet it can result in greater health, wealth, and joy for yourself and your organization. While these issues may appear to be "organizational," the fact is that all organizations are made of the people who comprise them. Therefore, you are a critically important factor in change, and you do have the capacity, as a single person, to effect the change that needs to be made. Inspired individuals can spark enormous shifts in seemingly immovable systems.

The first step in making a difference is to get in touch with your intention. Making it personal and not abstract can help to focus your efforts. Why do you care to change your experience of work and your work culture? How will these changes impact you? When you are clear about the benefits you will gain from your efforts, it will be easier to stick with your resolve to find solutions for what is not working for you.

Problems In The Workplace

If you work in a system or structure that doesn't allow you to use your talents, doesn't care about you personally, or doesn't help you align your purpose with your company's mission and vision, you may feel drained, frustrated, uninspired, and unwell. If you're feeling this way, you can't express your truth, or do your best work. The fear and aggression pervasive in dysfunctional work environments suppresses genuine communication, causes anxiety and stress, erodes engagement and motivation, destroys creativity, and inhibits collaboration and productivity. Over time, an oppressive work environment will cause health problems to multiply and employee turnover to soar. There is truly no sustainable upside to this type of workplace.

Employee engagement can be defined as "the emotional and functional commitment an employee has to their organization"[1]; employee *dis*engagement is an indicator of the need for an organization's leadership to connect authentically and meaningfully with its workforces. According to Gallup polls, in 2015, fewer than one-third of US workers were engaged positively in their jobs, and about 17 percent were actively disengaged, angry, and resentful.[2] The Bureau of National Affairs has calculated that $11 billion dollars are lost annually due to employee turnover,[3] and that same Gallup poll revealed that companies with engaged employees outperform those without by up to 202 percent!

The responsibility for this disengagement is shared by both employers and employees, and so is the solution. In this way, the work environment is very much like a romantic relationship: both parties have a shared responsibility in helping it thrive. And yet a working environment is comprised of many individuals, and the impact of a single unhappy individual in the workplace has great consequences for the whole. Even one unhappy person in a work group or department can be the source of a virus of negativity.

To find the most effective solution to this problem, each of us must discover the point in the system where we can be effective, which may depend on whether or not you have a managerial role. In order to help shift a situation, we must be willing to open ourselves up to the reality we find ourselves in, and remain tender and strong as we determine how we can make a difference. You don't need to be a manager to lead change, but if you are in a leadership role you are in a particularly strong position to help your employees feel genuinely happy and engaged. You can help them to find meaning in their work, recognize their accomplishments on a regular basis, and connect to the company vision by translating strategic goals into personal goals.

Lack of Motivation and Incentive

If you were drawn to this book, it is likely that you don't spring out of bed each weekday morning excited about work. As noted above, the current Gallup engagement survey reports that 68 percent of American workers are disengaged, or, in the words of comedian George Carlin, "Most people work just hard enough not to get fired and get paid just enough money not to quit." This unfortunate reality reflects a lack of inspiration in current work culture, and also a lack of imagination on the part of leadership to offer what motivates and energizes.

A paycheck is important, of course, but if you place even greater value on personal connection, community, meaningful work, peer recognition, and a career path that includes personal growth, you are in the majority. When these human factors are missing, the company misses out on contributions of creativity, collaboration, innovation, and loyalty. The stress and burnout from the lack of personal connection takes a toll.

There are a few important questions for you to consider regarding taking responsibility for your own motivation and connection to your work: Do you truly understand your company's mission and vision? Do you have clarity on your personal values and vision? And do your coworkers and leaders know or care about your personal vision and mission? These questions really matter, because if your personal vision and company vision don't have resonance and you are not being encouraged or mentored to establish this clarity and connection, confusion and frustration will ensue. If no one has shown interest in understanding what fires you up, or in aligning your work with your strengths and interests, the disconnect between your goals and the company's goals can be enormous and de-motivating.

So what can you do to turn this around? There is actually a lot in your control, even if you have determined that there is a complete disconnect between yourself and your company. As a first step, consider being an agent in bridging this clarity gap. You can start by adopting an attitude of curiosity about your current situation. The time you put into reconnecting with your reasons for being at your workplace in the first place can result in huge rewards for you and those you touch. It may be that you are only at your current job because you need the money to pay your bills. Perhaps you originally felt a real connection to the mission or vision you thought your work represented, and somewhere along the way the flame went out. Either way, reconnecting with your heart and why you show up to work each day is a spark for re-engagement. Your clarity may even help reinvigorate your colleagues by inspiring them to ask themselves this same simple question.

A Reactive, Unkind Culture

Some pain will be present in the workplace even in the best of cultures, because as individuals, in times of personal struggle, loss, and sadness, we bring our suffering to work with us. Pain and hurt is normal and human, and when it is acknowledged in a healthy culture it can be healing and can bring a team closer. In fact, a culture that allows you to bring all of yourself, including personal grief, to work is one that embraces the type of compassion that instills loyalty and dedication.

There is another, problematic type of pain we need to address both personally and systemically, however: the pain that occurs in a toxic culture where colleagues or the leaders in your group are unreasonably and consistently critical and unkind. Although it may be helpful to know that behavior like this often results from the personal insecurity or emotional immaturity of the "tyrant," that doesn't mean it won't still dramatically affect your feelings, as well as the culture of the company. If you work with individuals who express themselves in any of the following ways, you will need to draw upon your own leadership, emotional, and communication skills in order to begin to resolve this toxic climate for yourself and others.

Toxic behaviors:
- Excessive emotionality and reactivity
- Coldness and emotional distance
- Unreasonable expectations for productivity and goals
- Conflict avoidance
- Unwillingness to listen to others
- Lack of empathy and support
- Poor communication
- Aggression or intimidation[4]

One of my clients, Joe, worked for a mid-sized, privately owned manufacturing company where aggression and intimidation characterized the CEO's go-to style. Said CEO frequently berated his employees, both behind their backs and to their faces. He even treated the clients in the same hostile manner whenever they asked for something he considered to be outside of the contract they'd agreed to—and you can imagine how that was affecting business.

In meetings (which were rarely held, because the CEO undervalued communication), the CEO was unwilling to listen to others and often withheld pertinent information from his executive team. The overall climate was one of negativity, as the CEO's behavior was echoed by most of his subordinates toward their own team members. A trickle-down effect common in these kinds of environments was occurring.

Joe, however, was able to forge a different relationship with the CEO than anyone else on the team had. He practiced mindfulness both at home and on-the-spot at work, and through his practice found the personal confidence to not fear his CEO. Despite the negativity in his work environment, he genuinely liked the type of work the company was doing, and he decided to continue finding a way to move forward in his job. His regular mindfulness practice helped him develop the excellent emotional and communication skills necessary to create a healthy and honest relationship with his boss. The result was that he was treated with respect and had the opportunity to rectify many of the CEO's emotionally damaging exchanges within the company and externally, with clients.

While at times this role of arbiter felt overwhelming for Joe, he found a satisfaction in what he was able to accomplish and overcome at work. The skills he used to dilute some of the toxicity at his workplace were the same applications of mindfulness and compassion that you will be exploring for yourself. This is a worst-case scenario, and still it points out the power of one individual to positively affect a work environment. You are the key to change in your system, and no matter what the prevailing climate, you have the power to change your personal interactions. Start by envisioning a positive alternative for your work experience; then, take steps to make that vision a reality.

No Time or Space for Reflection, Creativity, and Recharging

In some workplaces, it is unacceptable not to be engaged in activity every moment. In fact, many of us, either by demand or by habit, are on call 24/7 by mobile phone, pager, or computer.

Some organizations have begun to recognize that an "always on" culture is not actually helpful. Sony Pictures, for example, discovered that adopting practices such as having employees shut down their cell phones for periods of time each day resulted in higher productivity.

Of course, we are not always in charge of how our time is spent. According to a report from the Center for Creative

Leadership, 52 percent of senior managers are interrupted every thirty minutes.[5] Clearly, this makes it difficult to focus on what is important. Ultimately, our efforts to change these time- and space-related workplace issues must involve interpersonal agreements; our teams and organizations must also engage in these new behaviors if we are to successfully engage in them ourselves.

The sheer amount of information we all process on a daily basis is also overwhelming, and the problem is particularly acute in the growing sphere of knowledge industries, which includes areas such as technology and professional services. In 2010, a LexisNexis survey revealed that white-collar employees spend more of their time receiving and managing information than doing their job. Many of the respondents of that survey said they felt that they were getting close to a point where they could not absorb any more data.[6]

It turns out that most Americans are preoccupied with work too much of the time. Intuitively we sense that perpetual busyness is not the equivalent of productivity, but research data now demonstrates that relaxing the brain and even indulging in a bit of daydreaming is necessary for optimal brain function. We need downtime and mental space during the day in order to make connections between events, allow inspiration and creativity to arise, and achieve our highest levels of productivity. In a fascinating article in *Scientific American* entitled "Why Your Brain Needs More Downtime," Feris Jabr cites neuroscientific research that proves that an occasionally idle mind is necessary for consolidating working memory, forming our sense of self, enhancing creativity, and integrating information.[7]

One of the ways we can actively create mental space for reflection, creativity, and recharging is by introducing regular short periods of meditation into our day. In fact, mindfulness meditation is a key ingredient in shifting a great many of the dysfunctional habits in our lives and organizations. You can easily take this step, which is simple to learn, and that first step will lead to a practice.

When it comes to turning around a painful situation, everyone can be a leader. Your leadership in managing your relationships, challenges, failures, disappointments, and success with equanimity and grace is the starting point for solving the systemic problems we face in the workplace. Meditation will lead to learning how to manage your emotions and actions in service of the greater vision you hold and share with your company. You will "be the change you wish to see," and become an example for others to emulate.

Your Important Role

Healthy interactions in the workplace will necessarily involve a network of interconnected individuals, activities, and policies—but any change you want to see in the world begins with you. If what you wish to accomplish involves influencing the world and events in which you participate, especially at your workplace, the first step begins with getting to know yourself. This is an exploration, at all levels, of what you are capable of imagining and willing to execute. It means dissolving the dysfunctions that you experience or initiate where possible, whether you are a CEO or mailroom clerk. You can take responsibility for understanding your own behavior, and lead the way for others.

Here are some very pointed questions to ask yourself: *Who am I? What do I think? Am I what I think? Am I aware of my thinking?* The answers to these fundamental questions are not clear-cut, of course, but what we believe to be true when we contemplate them is important to how we lead our lives.

Exercise: What Do You Think?

Take a minute to jot down what comes to mind when these questions are posed, and do so before you read further:

> Who am I?
> What do I think?
> Am I what I think?
> Am I aware of my thinking?

Take a moment to look back at these questions later, too. You may be surprised at how, after reading this book, your answers may change.

As you explore your sense of self, it's key to consider that the *you* that you are investigating may be much bigger and different than you were anticipating. This is not something I'm asking you to believe; it is something that you can only experience. When you open up to this possibility, it also opens the door to an underlying, wise space of innate goodness, kindness, and strength—one that will form a foundation for your vision and actions that exists underneath your surface thoughts. This possibility—that you might have capacities and power beyond how you now view yourself—may help you to take a deep breath and bravely look at what you are currently thinking and being.

Meeting Your Inner Critic

Have you ever experienced wanting to be different or more than what you think you are? What would it mean if you could accept and embrace who you truly are? This is an inquiry I have put to many clients who suffer from not really believing in themselves and their inherent goodness and worthiness over the years. A lack of self-esteem can be the root cause of many unhealthy and limiting behaviors at work, both for us and for those who affect us. Some signs of low self-esteem include excessive bragging and putting others down, always needing to have the last word in order to feel validated, or predicting failure rather than success before a task is even completed. All of these reactive behaviors are disruptive to work flow and can be addressed with personal awareness and a supportive environment.

Many people I counsel feel a sense of being a fraud when talking about their work or accomplishments, even if they are highly successful in the eyes of society. This sense of not being good enough can stop anyone from taking bold action in life. Holding yourself back in this way can be a great loss, because you have genuine wisdom, and you actually hold the answers that others need to hear.

Recognizing a lack of confidence in yourself can help you develop empathy for some of the negative behaviors your colleagues may exhibit at work, mentioned above, when they are feeling insecure about their worth and authority. It's important to recognize thoughts and behaviors that stem from a sense of unworthiness in ourselves, and also to create an environment of encouragement and empowerment for others so that we can thrive in a positive way together.

Your Two Selves

Through my explorations over the years, I have identified two facets of being: my "personal self" and my "vast self." I would like to invite you also to consider yourself in these two ways. Engaging with these two layers of life experience offers a path to being genuine, a path to being fully yourself. These two intersecting aspects of you contain all the material you need to effect meaningful change, and to connect with your innate goodness, the goodness of others with whom you have relationships, and the goodness and potential of the larger group, organization, and society.

Your Personal Self

The personal self is the person to whom you are referring to when you say "me." This aspect of self is also known as our ego, or sometimes our personality. We are pointing to the ordinary sense of self that is our day-to-day identity in life. While not the ultimate core of who we are, we absolutely need a healthy personal self as we engage with others on our journey of life. In this domain it is essential to identify and stay true to your unique strengths, values, and vision.

In terms of our day-to-day or personal self, in order to be successful, we have to embody a real sense of worthiness. Positive self-belief inoculates us against the slings and arrows of others. "Nobody can make you feel inferior without your consent," as Eleanor Roosevelt famously said. Yet even the strongest among us sometimes caves into doubts and self-judgment. The good news is that this quality of self-confidence is trainable. We can learn to be authentically, confidently, and uniquely our self!

DEVELOPING SELF-AWARENESS

The ancient practice of mindfulness meditation is now scientifically being shown to be an effective way of becoming self-aware, which is the key to being yourself. The practice of meditation is a method of quieting, focusing, and relaxing your mind. It is the key to self-awareness on a personal level, and will also be essential for exploration of our "vast self," where we delve below the surface of our personality. (The actual practice of mindfulness meditation will be explained in detail and fully discussed in Chapter 2.) As you deepen your self-awareness and self-knowledge, you simultaneously learn to let go of barriers to success that you have created in your own life.

UNMASKING YOUR INNER CRITIC

When you really listen to the voices in your head that tell you that other people are better than you, that you can't risk failure, that you need another credential before trying something new, ask yourself a question: Who is talking? Is it your parents, a teacher, a bully, or a former boss? Whoever it's coming from, it's not you—not originally.

When you were young you didn't set these limits on yourself. I remember a time when I was walking home from school around age seven, and a neighbor stopped me to talk. He asked me what I wanted to be when I grow up, and I instantly answered, "A famous actress." When he asked me what I would call myself, I responded, "Gigi" (my initials). In grade school I starred in every class play, and even wrote and performed my own music onstage. Somewhere along the way, however, around the time I hit middle school, I began to doubt myself. I don't remember who planted the seeds, but I no longer saw my dream as possible.

Sometimes the negative messaging is dramatic, like someone clearly telling you to "get realistic," but sometimes the influences on us are so subtle that we don't even realize we've taken on someone else's limiting beliefs. When you have a clear method for observing those voices in your head, it is much easier to deal with persistent doubting thoughts and to let them go. The memories or voices we hear are actually just stories, and when we see them as such they loosen their hold on us.

IDENTIFY YOUR STRENGTHS AND VALUES

Very often you underestimate your most powerful gifts because they come so naturally to you. It can be powerful to uncover what you may be unconsciously discounting. If you are a good listener and intuitively understand what someone is telling you, you can offer that clarity back to the person who feels uncertain, and that is a gift. If you find it easy to fix broken objects and find yourself always tinkering and making your environment function smoothly, that is a gift. The very things we do every day without any effort are often the key to how we can help others.

Exercise: What You Love

Make a list of what you love doing and what you are good at. Make another list of all your accomplishments and the skills you possess that people admire. Read this list and appreciate yourself!

Exercise: Articulate Your Values

A great way to discover your values, if you are not already familiar with them, is to think about people you admire. Bring to mind a person, either historical or a person you know well. Focus on one individual at a time when you do this exercise, so that you can really feel the qualities that they embody which affect you. Make a list of what you admire about that person. (Most often you share the values that they exhibit.)

Exercise: Personal Values Assessment

You can also take a Personal Values Assessment developed by the Barrett Values Center, available at www.HappierAtWork.com. This short quiz will provide a report and graph of your top values, how these may affect your behavior, and where you may want to focus attention, based on your values.

ACKNOWLEDGE YOUR WEAKNESSES

This may seem like a strange recommendation, but if you are measuring yourself against perfection, you're dooming yourself to failure. The flip side of knowing your strengths is knowing what you don't like to do, or what you don't do well, and what you may need help with. When you can be honest with yourself, you can relax and acknowledge that there are areas of life and business you don't even wish to master!

Over the past few years I have had to learn to give up trying to be and to do absolutely everything for myself. First, I tried to become proficient in all areas of my business. I took a long course on how to build my own WordPress website. I did accomplish the task, but it wasn't a great website. I also took courses on how to use social media and figured out how to better engage on Twitter, in addition to Facebook and LinkedIn, which I was already using. I now understand how to do it, but it takes so much time! I also created a marketing plan after taking an entrepreneurial business course and learned how to increase my income—but in the process, I began spending less and less time doing what I love to do and what I do best, which is teaching, coaching, training, and writing. When I realized what I wanted and needed to do, I returned to my core strengths. People began appearing in my life who wanted to team up with me to offer their skills—the very ones I had decided not to prioritize! It may seem like magic, but this kind of synchronicity has to do with developing clarity about what you do well and what you need to focus on in order to be effective and impact the world.

When you get clear and realize that there are skill areas you don't wish to master, you may find that cutting out these weaker aspects from your self-description helps you feel more authentic as you align with your strengths. Knowing both your strengths and weaknesses is key to good leadership and teamwork, as well as self-esteem. When you are in alignment with your strengths, you do your best work, and when you know your weaknesses, you can invite and include others to be part of the larger solution if it requires skill sets you have not mastered. Almost every project benefits from multiple points of view and diversified mastery. Teams have the potential to be creative and innovative when ideas can flow between individuals who feel confident enough in their own expertise to seek input from others.

Exercise: What I Can Let Go

Take some time now to list some skill areas that you are currently claiming as your own that you would prefer not to perform. Consider how focusing on what you do best will free you up to be a more powerful change maker.

PRACTICE SELF-COMPASSION

A growing body of research shows that self-criticism—"being mean to yourself"—when you make a mistake or fail actually sets you up for further failure. You are reinforcing negative thinking patterns and imagining a poor outcome rather than creating space for a fresh start.

Emma Seppala, Science Director of Stanford's Center for Compassion and Altruism Research and Education, discusses this in her book *The Happiness Track.* Seppala cites studies by psychologist Kristen Neff that suggest that the better approach is to treat ourselves as kindly as we would treat a friend or family member who has failed. Failing does not make us bad people; everyone has setbacks, and what we are going through is normal. We can let ourselves feel our feelings, but we should do so without giving in to them by reacting or beating ourselves up. We can acknowledge that what we are going through is really hard, and then send ourselves some compassion and love to get ourselves through it![8] (We will explore this topic in greater depth in Chapter 5.)

Exercise: Taking Action

You now have a lot of great information about yourself! You may have discovered that part of what "doesn't work" for you at work is a misalignment between what energizes you and the role you are playing in your workplace. Could you arrange a conversation with your immediate supervisor to explore a project or assignment that will bring more energy into your day? If you manage others, consider opening up this exploration of personal vision and value alignment with your team members.

Your Vast Self

This second aspect of self is a non-cognitive awareness. It is not something you know with your intellect—it is beyond our usual way of processing information—yet it is totally ordinary and available at the same time, as a sense of knowing or awareness itself. When you contact this aspect of who you are, you are uncovering and synchronizing with your deeper, more universal being, which gives energy, power, and magnetism to your every endeavor. Underneath your individual stories, dramas, hopes, and fears, you can touch into the goodness, wisdom, kindness, strength, and confidence that is actually already there as the essential "you." There is a deep well of experience available to humanity, and all of us have access to this pure potential. We just need to learn to tap into it.

COMING HOME

You might say that through the practice of meditation you are reconnecting to your natural "home." As you practice meditation and get familiar with your personal storylines, you are not only strengthening your ability to come back to a focus of your choice, you are learning to relax your mind, which brings it home to an experience free of discursive hope and fear. Home base is a space that has always been there—the space between your thoughts, between in-breath and out-breath, between one mood and another. You may recognize that space as the very thing you have been searching for in so many other ways. It is the peace and relaxation that you yearn for, and the clarity and knowing beyond book knowledge. It is the power to do what you dream of. In that original, basic space of being, you feel at home and connected to something bigger than your own version of life.

COMPASSION EXPANDS

As you become more relaxed and comfortable with yourself, you will learn not only how to be self-compassionate, but that everyone around you is being pretty darn hard on themselves also. You will become more caring and interested in others, and become a better listener who wants to make a difference. Being able to hear and be with another person with your whole being may be the most important outcome of becoming comfortable with yourself. As a person with openness and curiosity, you are much more likely to tune into what needs to be done for success to occur in any endeavor.

THINK BIG AND TRUST YOUR VISION

If your desire is to make a difference and help our world, you might follow the advice that Parker Palmer gave to students in his 2015 Naropa University Commencement Address: "Take on big jobs worth doing—jobs like the spread of love, peace, and justice. That means refusing to be seduced by our cultural obsession with being effective as measured by short-term results. Maintain faithfulness to your gifts, faithfulness to your perception of the needs of the world, and faithfulness to offering your gifts to whatever needs are within your reach."[9]

Our current commercial culture seems to value only the short-term bottom line and showing an immediate profit, and this often squashes our larger-than-self ideas. However, when we consider some of the bigger technology successes, such as Facebook or Twitter, we can see that investors did value a bigger vision and were willing to value those ventures highly without an immediate monetization model. Facebook did not turn a profit until 2009, five years after it was founded.

As a part of opening ourselves to a bigger perspective, perhaps we can imagine how we can lead change and inspire belief in our own innovations and not give in to fear of the unknown. This could mean starting a new company, coming up with a product idea, or even engineering a novel reorganization of how work is accomplished in your department or company.

Exercise: Your Big Dream

What is your big dream and vision? How can you apply your gifts to this vision? Write it down, and review it often.

CONNECT TO YOUR HEART AND
RIDE YOUR ENERGY

When you return to your home base, you are returning to your heart. This is the essence of the instruction to "be yourself." When you feel synchronized in your being, you connect to your heart as a powerful source of energy that radiates confidence, magnetizing people and situations. Learning to ride this energy is the path of a lifetime, and a journey well worth taking. You will be strengthening this connection as you progress through the activities in this book and as you continue to apply them in your daily life.

The very best way to be yourself is to put in the time to get to know both the "personal you" and the "vast you." The better you know yourself, the more you can exercise the important choices you have in any moment. As you practice being present and relaxed and making authentic choices, you will feel more and more integrated and aligned with yourself. You'll feel at ease, and begin to acknowledge your own value and worth. And as you radiate this simple confidence, it will become evident to others as well. Your kindness will be contagious. Your power will be real and unselfish, and you will have gained the ability to lead the life you have always imagined.

Your World and You

Let's step back a bit to the question asked earlier in this chapter, which relates to your important role in how you experience your life: "Am I what I think?"

In some ways, you are very much what you think in that when you think the same things over and over again, you create habits that become so familiar that you can start to think of them as who you are—part of your identity. This "me" identity begins to believe in and identify with these thoughts so that there seems to be no space between the thoughts, habits, actions, and experience of who we are. As life goes on, unless we do something to challenge this version of ourselves, we will recreate our life, moment by moment, in these same patterns.

On the other hand, you are *not* what you think. Your thoughts, beliefs, and even current interests are filters through which you experience your world. When you look at it this way, if you were able to change your filters—or do away with them altogether—you and your new experiences might surprise you!

Each thought you experience actually endures for only the briefest period of time. Thoughts arise and dissolve constantly, and you are always refreshing the version of yourself that thinks the same things over and over again. Understandably, perhaps, each of us is usually more comfortable with thinking and being what we know rather than the alternative, even if continuing on with the status quo does not bring us happiness. At some point a certain cycle of thoughts becomes somewhat self-sustaining. If you think the same thought over and over again, you strengthen the possibility that the thought will continue to assert itself. If you want to shift that pattern of being, you need intention and a way to interrupt that pattern.

In the next chapter, you will be introduced to a simple and effective approach to releasing unwanted thoughts and freeing your energy for other purposes—a method that involves looking inside yourself to discover how and what you think.

Your Worldview

You see the world uniquely, yet often through shared biases. You swim in a sea of views that greatly informs how your individual worldview filters are developed. These cultural norms are so pervasive that they are like the water fish swim in: we take them for granted. These systems of ideas are the environment within which our individual identities form, and they influence how we make sense of our existence. For those of us in the West, some of the pervasive ideas which inform our thinking include original sin, duality (right/wrong, good/bad, etc.), logic, primacy of the individual, competition, capitalism, and the notion that humans are at the top of the chain of life.

When we examine any of these ideas, or all of them, we can see the enormous effect they have on the decisions we make individually and as a society. For example, consider the American value of individualism. As a result of this perspective, Americans find it challenging to understand others' points of view. For individuals who were born in an East Asian culture, in contrast, the water is much different. Rather than individualism being primary, their view is more holistic and interpersonal. In a study done by the University of Chicago, for example, Chinese subjects were much more adept than individualistically oriented Americans at determining another person's perspective.[10]

Culture as Story

The culture we swim in is passed down as a story—one that is told to us and that we then tell ourselves and believe. People, families, groups, nations, and humanity all have stories. We are simultaneously embedded in multiple cultural stories. Our personal culture is sometimes called our "MO," or modus operandi. Relational culture involves how we habitually interact with partners and family, and it extends to our work colleagues, though work culture itself is a separate entity. We live within a national culture, and ultimately our shared human culture. In each of these aspects of our lives, we are largely unaware and at the mercy of invisible forces that dramatically affect our behavior. But you can learn to make the invisible visible—and in doing so, you can gain the power of choice regarding how you live your life and how your life affects your world.

When culture is a way of thinking, behaving, or working that exists in a place or organization, it is expressed as the set of shared attitudes, values, goals, and practices. In simplest terms, it can be understood as "the way things are done around here." Of course, an organization is not a being. It does not think or hold values. This organizational culture, therefore, is an invisible force that is both shaped by and reflective of the values, beliefs, and behaviors of the individuals who comprise the collective. The "personality" or culture of a business is largely determined by the values, beliefs, and behaviors of its current and past leaders and is reflected in the structures and procedures, systems, and policies of the organization.

When we examine the culture of an organization (or individual) we can see that there are both conscious and unconscious values at play. Those values can be identified as either positive or potentially limiting. Positive values promote openness, collaboration, trust, honesty, and integrity. Potentially limiting values are fear-based beliefs that have the effect of limiting the flow of information and ideas, reducing cooperation, reducing creativity, and causing frustration throughout the organization.

The Power of a Positive View

What you believe shapes your life, both mentally and physically. In one surprising study of how belief affects our bodies, Dr. Becca Levy from the Yale School of Public Health found that individuals with a more positive view of aging tended to live seven and a half years longer than those with more negative views of aging.[11]

If you are weight conscious, consider a study conducted by Harvard psychologist Ellen Langer, who discovered that your perception of your activity is more important than your activity level itself in regards to weight loss. In a study done with cleaning crews in a hotel, she found that workers were very physically active, but most did not consider what they were doing to be exercise. Langer broke the group of eighty-four maids into two groups. One group was told that their activity level already met the surgeon general's definition of an active lifestyle. The other group was told nothing. When the women's measurements were taken one month later, the team of researchers was surprised by what they found. "In the group that had been educated, there was a decrease in their systolic blood pressure, weight, and waist-to-hip ratio—and a 10 percent drop in blood pressure."[12] Langer attributes these results to a placebo effect: your belief that you are exercising makes your body behave as if it is. Those who did not believe that they were exercising did not experience the benefits.

Let's turn to another underlying belief in the West, original sin, which has a pervasive influence on us. This concept that there is something inherently bad at our core that needs to be fixed, that we are not essentially good enough as we are, causes us great pain. While this understanding of original sin may be a distortion, nonetheless, it can lead to judging ourselves as falling short in every imaginable way. To cure this feeling you may feel the need to buy something new, or eat something different, or find a new partner or spouse. You may think you are too fat, too thin, not smart enough, not good enough, not wealthy enough, and so on. Furthermore, when you judge yourself harshly, it is hard to see others without similarly judging them. The world we experience is a mirror of our state of mind, and we notice others' flaws before we notice their goodness.

What if you could look at the world through the lens of a new story? What if you could know through personal experience that you are inherently good, wise, strong, and kind? That would change dramatically the narrative that you tell yourself and share with others; in fact, it would change how you view society altogether.

As you take the journey this book offers, you may find that a new story of your life is emerging, one of original purity, which offers fantastic possibilities for shifting your life, relationships, work environments, and intractable societal issues. You will explore how to develop and deepen your self-awareness and social awareness, and how you can make a profound difference in your life, your workplace, and our world. With mindful awareness, self-compassion, and compassion for others, you will be the key to the changes you wish to see and be.

CHAPTER 2:

Un-Stress Your Workday

If only you could get a moment of peace and quiet! Of course you want that, overwhelmed as you are with information, deadlines, and regular interruptions, not to mention your constant waterfall of mental chatter. In fact, the number one question I hear in interviews with coaching clients and meditation students is: How can I silence my mind?

Quiet has long been known to be an essential need. The seventeenth-century mathematician, inventor, and philosopher Blaise Pascal summed up the importance of silence by saying, "All of man's misfortune comes from one thing, which is not knowing how to sit quietly in a room." What does that phrase point to? What could it mean to know how to sit quietly in a room?

As you consider the answer to this question, think about how you normally spend your time before, during, and after work. At work, there is the challenge and constant pull of multitasking—e-mails and texts, conference calls and meetings, and coworkers needing your attention. Outside, with the honking of cars and the roaring of lawn mowers and leaf blowers, silence is hardly present. Indoors and out, we are surrounded by a deafening and constant roar of sound. No wonder so many of us question how to find any silence in our modern lives. It has become critically important that we discover personally how to be present and effective in the midst of this tremendous external input—and nowhere is the situation more challenging than when we are trying to focus, lead, and innovate at work.

The Value of Silence

Noise pollution and information overload impedes creativity, limits our focus, and increases stress. As a result of research done by Harvard Business School's Leslie Perlow, many companies such as IBM, Intel, U.S. Cellular, and Deloitte & Touche are now implementing "quiet time" periods when workers are protected from interruptions in order to focus on their work at hand.[13] During the "quiet time" in Perlow's study at a high-tech software company, individuals were banned from all messaging and phone contact for four hours in the morning. When given time to concentrate in this way, the workers' performance significantly improved.[14] Although this research was done with engineers, it is safe to say that some period of time where e-mail, phone, and web access are limited would be a welcome break for anyone in a busy office environment. Creativity and new ideas can spring into being when we provide space in our day and minds for that to happen.

Micro-Practice

Step away for a moment. When you feel overwhelmed by chaos at your desk or with others, try literally walking away and find a few moments to be alone, take a few deep breaths, and regain your sense of balance.

A neuroscience study on the effects of silence provides support for the importance of silence in memory and learning. In 2013, Duke scientist Imke Kirste was studying the effects of sound on the brains of adult mice. She was studying different types of sound inputs to discover how they stimulated brain cell growth in mice, including the sounds of baby mice, white noise, and silence. Much to her surprise, what she found was that new brain cells formed in the hippocampus area of the mice's brains (the part of the brain associated with memory involving the senses) in response to the two hours of silence each day, rather than to either of the other sound inputs. The new neurons that developed in response to silence became functioning and integrated into that area of the brain.[15] In other words, in this experiment the absence of sound stimulated learning. Although this is a preliminary finding, it has interesting implications for the sensory overwhelm we currently experience, and the importance of periods of silence to allow us to consolidate memory and learning.

In 2001, Marcus Raichle, a neuroscientist at Washington University, published a paper describing brain function's "default mode"—a term for all the scanning and evaluating activity and processing going on in our brains (in the prefrontal cortex) while we are not engaged in focused activity.[16] In 2013, neuroscientist Joseph Moran wrote in *Frontiers of Human Neuroscience* that the default mode can be associated with times of quiet self-reflection. He observed that at times of quiet both outside and within ourselves, when we are not performing goal-oriented tasks, we can find meaning and better understand our self in relation to the world.[17]

All this points to the need for us to find a balance at work between being always "on" and learning to take a pause. Being still and quiet can both help us focus and give us a much-needed break from constant input.

Learning to Pause And Focus

Other than shutting off our electronic devices and shutting the door to our office, experience and evidence tells us that there is only one place we can reliably turn to for peace and quiet—and that place is within our own being. We can train ourselves to be still and quiet, and each of us has access to that same deep source of inspiration that the greatest minds have tapped. When we re-learn how to quiet our minds to take a pause, or to focus our attention and concentrate, we are experiencing "knowing how to sit quietly in a room"—an ability that is widely considered to be one of the keys to happiness.

"But wait!" you might say. "Inside my own head is the loudest and craziest place of all, *especially* when I sit still and get quiet." This is true for many of us. The thoughts that tumble around in our minds, one after another, can seem like the loudest sound around, and as a meditation mentor I am constantly being asked for instructions on how to "shut off the thoughts." In my experience, however, shutting off the thoughts is not the way it works. The thoughts themselves are not the problem.

Learning *how to relate with thoughts* is a tremendous step we will explore on this journey to discovering your inner power—

but first, let's take some steps to slow down and connect with both your external and internal environments. In the absence of your usual activity, you have the opportunity to courageously look at and listen to what is filling your mind.

Exercise: Mini-Adventures

Here are a few mini-adventures you can embark upon outside of work that may give you some incredible insights. You might want to take some notes in a journal after trying out these activities:

1. Take a walk without wearing earphones. Pay attention to what you are seeing, hearing, and feeling. Try focusing on one sense field at a time. What do you smell? What physical sensations are you feeling? What do you see? What do you hear?

2. Prepare yourself a meal and sit down to eat it without reading, listening to music, or watching TV. Notice the flavors, the textures of the ingredients, the sounds of your chewing. What are you feeling?

3. Sit down in your home or out in nature and do nothing. Just breathe and notice. Do this for at least five minutes.

4. Spend a day without using your cell phone, iPad, computer, or any electronic device. Notice how that makes you feel. Notice how many times you think about reaching for one of those devices.

Mindfulness

The above exercises provide you with an opportunity to experiment with mindfulness. Mindfulness is a state of active, intentional attention on the present moment. When you pay attention to an object you are observing or an activity you are performing, you are utilizing your mind in an important and fundamentally empowering manner. Being able to place and hold your mind on what you choose is a basic human ability—an innate faculty—but like biceps, unless you exercise this muscle it will become weak and not all that useful. Your faculty of mindfulness needs to be acknowledged and strengthened if it is to help you with focus, and with being present to the moment that is unfolding.

Your life reveals itself in the present. This seems like an obvious statement, yet how often are you are caught up in your thoughts and living in a fantasy triggered by memories or wishes for the future? Until you develop the ability to focus at will, opportunities for action will continually slip away from you. The basic point of a mindfulness practice is to relate to what is actually happening in the fullest way. We do this by creating a disciplined mind that is able to stay where we place it.

An undisciplined mind pulls your attention from one thing to another. Mindfulness, when practiced over time, develops your ability to be fully engaged in the present moment and activities. An immediate benefit of starting to train in mindfulness is that as you become aware of your thoughts, you notice how your experience is colored by your expectations. When you can see through your own stories and interpretations of any situation, you are able to see more directly what is actually occurring. The person who seems to be angry with you when you ask a question may actually be frustrated with their own inability to complete a task, and not even thinking about you. Your assistant who appears lazy and inattentive may have been up all night with a sick child. Being able to sort fact from fiction will help you avoid needless stress and worry over situations that are not what they seem. Mindfulness meditation is a simple technique you can make a part of your day that will bring you direct results in all of your work and business activities. When you can drop into your work and exchanges with others fully, you will enjoy enhanced focus and effectiveness, increased ability to communicate clearly, and sharpened critical thinking and decision-making. All of these everyday work competencies are improved by the increased attention, clarity, insight, and understanding that result from being fully engaged in the moment and able to respond accurately.

Micro-Practice

Decide to be present. At the start of your work day, when you first sit down at your desk, pause and set this intention in your mind before you dive into your work.

Practicing Mindfulness Meditation

My close friend Tom recently shared with me that he doesn't meditate because he feels it will drain away too much of his energy. That surprised me, so I dug a little bit deeper, and he revealed that he believes that the point of meditation is to empty his mind of thoughts. I agreed with him that this particular goal would be exhausting and nearly impossible for most of us—and then I explained that it is *not* the point of meditation. Emptying one's mind of all thoughts is indeed a temporary *state* that is attainable by some highly seasoned meditators, but it is just that: a state. And such a state, if reached, eventually dissipates, leaving pain in its wake. By contrast, mindfulness is a way of being that becomes stronger and more available to you in all moments of life as you practice applying it.

Meditation, which focuses on returning attention lightly to the breath, trains you to develop the ability or "muscle" of mindfulness and awareness—to be able to focus on what is happening without being pulled away by distractions. You will be using this practice as a central tool to thrive at work and help to create a healthier and more productive workplace.

While learning this discipline you will undoubtedly get "hooked," or pulled away by thoughts, emotions, stories, hopes, and fears. When you notice that this has happened, it's important not to judge yourself as having done anything wrong. You can simply note that occurrence as "thinking," and then return your awareness to your breath. Actually, this very activity— noticing that you have been pulled away and then exercising the awareness and intention to gently return to your breathing—is the practice itself. It is the noticing and returning that will build your mindfulness muscle, and over time you will find it easier and easier to stay in the moment.

As you continue to strengthen your mindfulness muscle, you will reap multiple benefits. Being able to maintain or quickly return your focus to the proposal you are writing or the conversation you having with your colleague will not only make you more productive, it will actually give you more of the scarcest resource in your day: attention! We are information overwhelmed and attention deprived, so the practice of mindfulness can have a huge impact on our effectiveness.

Micro-Practice

Connect with your senses. When you feel yourself getting lost in a train of thought, bring your full attention back to simple activities like washing your hands, opening the door, and hearing a phone ring. When you are waiting for a meeting, you can take those few moments to tune into your breathing.

The exercise below is a description of the formal practice of meditation, which you can practice at home, at your desk, or on a work break. Once you establish a full practice, you will find that you are able to become present by taking even one mindful breath.

Practice:
Mindfulness Breathing Meditation

Posture—Like a Mountain

- The spine is upright, with a natural curve.
- The hands are resting on the thighs.
- The arms and shoulders are relaxed.
- The chin is slightly tucked.
- The eyelids are half-closed, with a soft gaze.
- The face and jaw are natural and relaxed.
- If you're sitting on a cushion, the legs are loosely crossed. If you are sitting on a chair, keep both feet firmly on the floor.

(continued on next page)

(continued from previous page)

Breathing—Natural

- Rest in the present by placing your mind on your body breathing.
- Feel your chest or belly rising and falling, or air coming and going from your nostrils.
- Your breathing happens moment by moment, always in the present.
- Appreciate how your breathing is intimately connected to being alive.

Thoughts—Energy of the Mind

- When thoughts arise, they are not a problem; if you are present, you can just watch them arise and dissolve.
- If a thought, emotion, or story pulls you away from your focus on your breathing, just notice that and return gently, without judgment, to feeling your body breathing.

Meditation is Natural

If meditation is the act of intentionally placing our mind on an object, we actually are always meditating. Usually, however, we focus on "me," our habitual thinking mind, as our chosen object—and our habitual thinking mind is usually wandering from one fantasy to another, living in the past (often regret), or future (hope and fear). During our workday, we may "meditate" on the stupidity of those who don't agree with us, or get lost in anxiety about meeting a deadline. We don't seem to have a lot of control over where our mind is focusing. In mindfulness meditation, you train your mind by giving it a place to rest in the present moment: on your breathing. When you notice thoughts, you let them go, gently returning to your breath. It doesn't matter if these thoughts are good or bad, you simply come back home without judgment. You are learning to let go of ties to your confused mind, and to rest in your clear, stable, underlying vast self.

Micro-Practice

Take mindful breaths. Any time you find you are overwhelmed, tense, or unable to focus is a good time to pause and take a few mindful breaths. Simply sit up in your chair and get in touch with your body and your breathing. Relax your shoulders, your eyes, and your jaw. Breathe deep into the belly, in through your nose and out through your mouth. That's it! After three to seven breaths, you can return to your task with renewed focus and calm.

Discovering Inner Space

When you feel overwhelmed, you might observe yourself wishing for some space. When we are not at ease, we often feel squeezed for both time and space. As this practice of mindfulness becomes a natural discipline, you'll find that you can contact a space that is vast, clear, tender, and surprisingly familiar. The background space that has room for all our wild thoughts is always there. This space is familiar to us because it is the ground of our being, that very feeling and place to which we are always trying to return. It is the source of joy and happiness that cannot be found outside of us.

This open field of possibility is the ultimate space of meditation, and it is also the foundation and resultant state of our journey to wholeness as human beings. As we develop our capacity for mindfulness, we are able to return more and more often to dip into this deep well of unconditioned goodness that is our birthright. With growing self-awareness, this space of calm energy and wisdom can infuse our lives and leadership. Let's explore this basic terrain of our being, and then we will have a chance to see how this knowledge operates to open our hearts and minds at work.

Dispelling Confusion

The first step to connecting with our true nature is to develop the capacity to not be so distracted. We can think of the wide-open sky as an analogy for our vast self. Thoughts arise naturally and constantly in this space of our mind, just like wisps of clouds that arise and evaporate in a blue sky. Non-distraction is when we can rest easily with the blue sky, aware of but not ruled by our thoughts.

In the wide-open sky, the sun is always shining, providing illumination and warmth unconditionally. Even when the sun is covered by the thickest cover of clouds, we don't doubt that it is there in the sky, and even when we are experiencing a cold rainstorm, we still know that the sun's basic nature is light and warmth. This is because we have certainty that we have experienced the sun.

In the case of your basic nature, you may not be sure whether you have experienced the clear, awake, and compassionate nature of your mind before, but every one of us has at some point. Most of us remember it as a sense of peace—the happy moments we've had, perhaps randomly, that we may sometimes wonder how to "recapture" or get back to. But even if we have glimpsed this reality, we don't know how to stabilize it, and confusion seems to cover over this basic nature and run our life.

HOW WE DISTORT

What is this confusion? It's a layer of ordinary perception where we experience our self as separate from our vast self, our basic nature, and our natural sense perceptions. We distort the utter simplicity of things as they are by viewing our life through complex filters composed of past experiences, preconceptions, and beliefs inherited from parents, teachers, and religion.

These views of life are inextricably tied to our emotional states. We feel separate from our world, and based on our evaluation of what is occurring, we have an emotional reaction to our perception. We passionately desire to possess and own our perception, or we aggressively wish to push it away—or we ignore it altogether.

As human beings, we all encounter this challenge. In order to know the fullness and truth of what is happening in each moment, we need to first be aware of how we might be distorting reality.

Scientists call the tendency to interpret information in a way that confirms our own preconception "confirmation bias." This is similar to the description found in meditation traditions, where this experience is considered to be ignorance caused by the formation of our habitual ways of perceiving. An old Buddhist parable tells the tale of a man walking home one evening. He sees a snake on the path in front of him and jumps and turns away with a thumping heart, alert for danger. Then, looking more closely, he realizes he was wrong; the "snake" is actually a piece of rope! Relieved, he laughs at himself, and then, as he steps over it, he realizes that the rope is in fact a valuable string of pearls. This is a story about confused perception, something that we act out in our own way myriad times each day.

OUR STORIES

We are constantly telling ourselves stories. A powerful example was circulated on the web a few years ago when a businessman wrote a blog about his experience on a commuter train a father and his six young children were also riding. The children were wild and unruly, teasing each other and running up and down the aisles. The businessman got more and more outraged that the father was just ignoring their behavior and he finally turned to the man and said, "Can you please control your children?" The man raised his gaze from his lap and said, "I am so sorry, we are just returning from their mother's funeral, and none of us know how to handle it." In an instant, the judging mind of the businessman flipped to compassion, and he experienced the situation completely differently.

One of the most powerful effects of mindfulness meditation practice is that it allows us to see our own stories and to become familiar with them in the safe environment of meditation practice. This is important, because until we see that we are weaving our feelings and perceptions into our stories about what we observe, we just think we are experiencing "reality." With increased awareness, however, we can observe how these types of distortions arise in endless ways throughout our day. For instance, when we see someone we haven't met across a room, if they resemble someone we know, we may unconsciously project the known person's qualities onto them. If we are in a meeting and someone disagrees with us, we may form a negative opinion of them and stop listening to what they have to share. If we read an e-mail too quickly, we may miss an important line in the content, resulting in miscommunication or unnecessary anxiety. Worse, we may draft a response to the e-mail based on that mistaken view. If we have reviewed similar distortions arising as thoughts during our meditation, however, we will catch them before we completely believe them in our daily life.

Your emotional/mental experience has myriad expressions. When you see others getting what you wanted, such as a promotion or a project you know you deserved, it may engender jealousy or greed, and when things don't go how you planned, you may get angry or hurt. The emotional turmoil you experience is constantly changing, and it may contribute to a further feeling of confusion and lack of control over your life. In all of these scenarios, the subject is you, and the object is something or some experience that you are having a relationship with. Interestingly, in the scenarios painted above, and in our own day-to-day lives, our experiences are not fresh but rather a patterned replay of what we expect to happen based on what has happened to us before, in the past.

There is an alternative available to us. In the gap between thoughts, in the freshness of a moment, when you totally relax into being your true self, the confusion disappears. This is why you need to take a breath and stop, allowing this possibility to be experienced.

The Laziness Factor

The laziness factor comes into play when you "space out" at work. Being present, after all, takes a lot of effort. The present is said to be the only moment that is real, the only time when we can make a choice and influence our lives, but each of us has created elaborate strategies for avoiding the present and the potent responsibility it implies. If we are present for our life, we can't blame others for our decisions and the outcomes of our choices. Being awake and aware can feel too real, too overwhelming. Our societal and work cultures conspire with us to create endless distractions, and we develop strategies of avoidance.

When we feel our life directly, it is sharp, fresh, and on the dot. Often we feel lazy and don't want to be that directly engaged. Our laziness can take the form of two extremes: sluggishness or extreme busyness. When you are in the middle of a project and start roaming on Facebook, checking your e-mail, or standing around gossiping about others, for example, you are most likely avoiding being present.

Micro-Practice

Set reminders to be present. Try setting an alarm on your phone, perhaps a vibrating reminder. Notice what you are thinking or doing when the alarm goes off. Set appointments in your calendar to be mindful, and when those reminders pop up, take a mindful moment.

ACCEPTING THE CHALLENGE

You might also fool yourself that you are engaging with life by keeping yourself busy doing one task or another instead of addressing one that truly challenges you. Can you relate to the urge to clean up your inbox when you have an important and difficult letter to write? Either by wasting time or doing busy work, you are avoiding the potent present of your life—and if you can see this, you can do something about it!

It feels so good to recognize when you have been stalling and then attack the job at hand. An energy is released, ideas flow again, and you actually feel happier. This is not different from reengaging with a physical exercise routine; your self-esteem is boosted by the discipline, and energy is released from the activity itself. This can be an important boost to productivity in your day. Find where you are stalling and just jump in.

Exercise: Project List

Make a list of projects and tasks you have been putting off. Attach a completion date to each one.

Stress and How to Work with It

Mindfulness allows us to see things clearly, which in turn provides us with an instantaneous choice. Let things be as they are, or struggle against what is. Struggling against what is can be the source of much of the constant stress we experience. Letting things be as they are doesn't mean that you can't take action; it means you don't jump into *re*action, which actually cuts off your opportunity to make a meaningful response. That reactivity triggers more stress and the cycle continues.

Often we don't like the situation that is unfolding. Maybe your company is being bought and tremendous change is occurring. Perhaps sales are slow and you are asked to participate in layoff decisions. If you don't have the ability to change the larger situation itself, you can reduce your stress by directly connecting with what is occurring and considering your options. When you actually relate directly, without letting your habitual stories interfere, something amazing happens: time seems to slow down, or you seem to have more opportunity to be present to your experience. You now have the opportunity to choose how to move forward based on that clear seeing. You may experience a relaxation that is connected to the state of non-aggression, or lack of struggling.

Work stress is on the rise. The Harris Work Stress Survey puts the current percentage of people who are stressed by something at work in the US at 83 percent![18] Often we contribute to our own stress in ways that we can begin to recognize and control. What are you struggling with? What do you filter or distort in your work experience that could be creating a sense of struggle? That is a question worthy of examination. The best way to find the answer is to sit down and spend time with yourself. The practice of sitting meditation is the way that I have chosen to look at my own thinking process and discover what, in fact, are the recurring filters, the patterned thoughts and stories I tell myself, that are obscuring my direct perception. I have discovered that I struggle and create stress by telling myself I don't have enough time or don't know enough, or that something is too difficult, when in fact none of these thoughts are usually true once I look directly at the situation I am avoiding.

Exercise: Where I Struggle

Look at the recurrent ways that you struggle. When you have identified a few, try turning them around. For instance, if you always are telling yourself, "I don't have enough time," try saying to yourself, "I have enough time for this." See how shifting the story can shift your perception.

You may be afraid of looking at your own thoughts, patterns of behavior, and beliefs. You may fear that you won't like what you find if you slow down enough to actually hear the constant chatter that fills your mind day and night. It may not be easy at first to acknowledge that your repetitious thoughts have been controlling your behavior and experience, but the good news is that these thoughts are not you; they are simply thoughts that have no more substance than the imprint of a bird in the sky. Through the practice of meditation, we can learn to notice a thought arising and then let it dissolve without getting hooked by it. This takes some time to master, of course, and that is why meditation is also called practice.

We are practicing to develop the muscle of mindfulness and awareness so that we can bring ourselves back to the openness of our vast mind over and over again. We are learning to unhook from our personal triggers, with which we will become extremely familiar through the courageous activity of sitting down and looking directly at what arises in our mind. Then those very patterns can become friendly reminders to relax and let go, to let the sun of our being dissolve the storm clouds of confusion. When you are in that moment of returning, you are at one with your natural space and clarity. You have the ability to respond rather than react. Your actions are authentic and without aggression, and have a powerful, positive effect on your ability to lead and communicate genuinely.

Multitasking Can Also Be a Cause of Stress

When we multitask we think that we are accomplishing more than one thing at a time, but actually we are training ourselves in "inattention" because we are not able to focus on one thing at a time. Having so many balls in the air means we are literally juggling our attention, and training ourselves to do so. We may think that we can switch back easily to one-pointed focus, but as Stanford researcher Clifford Nass told NPR, "people who multitask all the time can't filter out irrelevancy. They're chronically distracted. They initiate much larger parts of their brain that are irrelevant to the task at hand."[19] Conducting ourselves in this way consumes more of our mental resources, wastes time, and ultimately makes us worse performers and leaders.

When we practice mindfulness, we are training ourselves to notice when we have become distracted and to return our awareness to the present-moment task. In a *Harvard Business Review* article called "The Focused Leader," Daniel Goleman points out that "focusing inward and focusing constructively on others helps leaders cultivate the primary elements of emotional intelligence. A fuller understanding of how they focus on the wider world can improve their ability to devise strategy, innovate, and manage organizations."[20]

As a leader, it is essential to learn to focus your own attention. First you train in self-awareness, focusing your attention inward. Then you develop the capacity to direct your focus to others, and the wider societal sphere.

The Neuroscience Of Mindfulness

For those of us who want to see scientific proof before we take up the practice of meditation, there are studies being done to provide just that. From these studies, the term "neuroplasticity" has emerged, which describes the ability of the mind to adapt and change as needed. You can train your mind to change and instill new ways of thinking that help you change for the better. In the past decade, due to both the need to understand how to reduce the ill effects of overstimulation and stress on mental and physical health and the improved technology that allows us to peer into the workings of the brain, the number of studies looking at the effect of mindfulness on our brains has multiplied exponentially. These studies have proven that the practice of mindfulness reduces stress, increases mental clarity and creativity, improves our cognitive performance overall, and increases happiness and well-being.

Mindfulness affects the brain in multiple ways. Two of the most powerful are attention regulation and emotional regulation. Attention regulation is important to us because it is the basic, first, and primary skill gained from mindfulness practice. In our busy, sensory-overloaded, digital world, the ability to sustain focus and return our attention to the subject of our choice is a skill critical to leadership and stellar performance at any level. The brain change that appears as a result of the development of attention regulation is a thickening of the anterior cingulate cortex (ACC). The journal *Perspectives on Psychological Science* reports that an increase in brain cells, and their connections to each other from meditation practice, enhances our ability to maintain attention while disregarding distractions. This learned skill is known as conflict monitoring or executive attention.[21]

Another powerful effect of mindfulness practice has to do with our emotional intelligence—our ability to remain open and aware to the present and whatever is happening non-judgmentally and without reactivity. This is important while dealing with challenging or unexpected situations, conversations, and individuals. If we can maintain our composure, our "cool," we can appraise a situation more objectively and locate the proper response. The prefrontal cortex, amygdala, and hippocampus are all involved in these processes. When this ability is developed, the communication between our more rational prefrontal cortex and more primitive amygdala (fight or flight response center) is strengthened. The prefrontal cortex is able to downregulate the amygdala, reducing the outpouring of hormones that cause us to have a panic response.

Some areas of the brain respond more quickly than others to meditation practice. One study published in *Perspectives on Psychological Science* showcased how, after only an eight-week meditation course, mindfulness meditators had an increase in left-sided anterior brain activation—the part of the brain that's been shown to be associated with feelings of happiness or well-being.[22] This result is an encouraging indicator that engaging in this practice can lead to powerful and meaningful stress reduction in a very short period of time.

At Aetna, the American health insurer, almost 15,000 employees have participated in at least one meditation or yoga course offered by the company—and the results have been fantastic. The participants reported, on average, a 28 percent reduction in stress levels and a 20 percent improvement in sleep quality. They also became more effective at work, measured as an increase of sixty-two minutes per week of increased productivity. Aetna valued this stress reduction to be worth $3,000 per employee per year; additionally, medical claims at the company dropped by 7.3 percent in 2012, saving the company another $9 million.[23] So we can see that real change happens in our brains as a result of meditation, and that real change is reflected in a healthier mind and body, with financial benefits flowing to the workplace that supports mindfulness.

CHAPTER 3:

Transform the Energy of Fear

We live in a fearful and anxious world. A feeling of uncertainty pervades many of our everyday encounters, and many of us feel a constant sense of unease. We experience fear in many forms: panic at bad news; overwhelm and inability to handle our lives; feelings of doubt and inadequacy; nervous and restless energy that won't let us relax; even deep sadness. It feels overwhelming to take a look at all of these groundless feelings, but if we don't look, we may miss the opportunity to not only shift but understand this powerful energy.

To understand the external stimuli to our anxiety, we need only to look at our common activities. Even travel, surrounded as it now is by fearful messages and exhortations, has become a traumatic experience. When you arrive at the airport, you are constantly reminded to watch out for danger at every turn. You are considered suspicious until proven innocent as you pass through the screening machines, and you'd better not make a joke on the security line or the reaction from the already-jittery agents might make you miss your flight.

If you are a parent, meanwhile, fears beyond concerns for a healthy baby start soon after conception. You're warned to get the unborn baby on the right preschool waiting lists or they won't have a chance of getting enrolled when the time comes. Then you're strongly encouraged to make sure they excel at least one extracurricular sport, and also make sure they develop a professional volunteer experience portfolio. This kind of pressure continues for parents all the way until college—and this anxiety is passed on to our children, who later bring these anxious patterns into their professional lives. The workplace mirrors the norms of our schools and society. Competition for class rank and college acceptance turns into competitive workplace behaviors. You may experience excessive competition for rank and resources within your department, or your company may even pit one department against another. This competition is often accompanied by fear, a wariness and distrust of one's colleagues and the unknown.

As a first step, this fear in the workplace needs to be acknowledged. If that step is not taken, little can be done. To illustrate this point: A few years ago, I was invited to a consultation with a large medical group in our city. They knew that they had a serious morale problem, and that it had to do with the relationship between the nursing staff and the physicians on staff. Management invited me in to create an uplifting experience, and asked me to hire some clowns for the event. I asked to meet with them first, to gather some more information in order to make a proposal.

As we talked, it became clear that the physicians were creating an atmosphere of intimidation for the nursing staff, and that trust and respect did not exist between these two essential parts of their organization. I suggested that as a part of our process, we create a survey that would allow all individuals to share their experiences, thinking that might help us find the best way forward.

At this point, the executive to whom I was speaking said, "And if the survey revealed the fear that you have been talking about, would we have to share those results?"

"I think that would be the best way to move forward," I said.

"No thank you," she said. "We don't want to open up that box. I think we'll be better off just hiring a clown to make people feel better."

This is a true story! So again, the first step to addressing fear in an organization is having the courage to acknowledge that it is there.

Causes of Fear at Work

Some of the fear we experience at work may be our personal emotional response to the world we live in. In the 1990s, the US Army war college introduced the acronym VUCA to describe the volatility, uncertainty, complexity, and ambiguity of our times. This all-pervasive source of anxiety is reflected in our workplaces, where the volatile, uncertain, and complex economics of our times are at play. The military is seeking solutions to VUCA, which includes research into implementing mindfulness meditation to combat stress and strengthen the cognitive functioning of active duty troops, and the results have been very promising. Mindfulness training has been shown to increase soldiers' ability to handle stressful and complex situations, and to lead to improvement of mood and enhanced ability to solve complex problems.[24]

At work, although you don't face the stress of actual battle, a primary source of fear-related stress may be embodied in the management culture. If your work culture is one of distrust and aggression, you may be experiencing a fear-motivated environment, and you may even be using these fear tactics as a motivator with those you manage as well. It is possible that "normal" where you work is an unconscious reflection of reactivity to fear and uncertainty. As such, it is important to take a close personal look at how you are affected by fear, and how you may be affecting others.

Exercise: Looking at Daily Fear

Take a look at how fear comes up for you on a daily basis at work. You might want to journal about this, and in re-reading, reflect on whether you may also employ any of those behaviors with others. Once the patterns of control-by-fear are revealed, they are easier to dismantle.

Change

Change is inevitable, and while we sometimes regard change as exciting, it also can be a source of discomfort or dread. Even the good news of a promotion can elicit fears, such as not being competent enough for the new post. You may be moving to a new department, and fear having to form new relationships and master new office politics. Or perhaps the word is out that your company is being acquired and layoffs are expected. Whatever the change, a good first step, once again, is to acknowledge that the change is happening. Next, write down what scares you about it. This is a mindful action that allows you to address your fear in the present moment. This also gets the worry out of your head and down on paper. I use this technique when I am awake in the middle of the night worrying about something that I can do absolutely nothing about. What I actually need to do is to get back to sleep so that I can handle the issue in the morning. Writing down what is going around and around in my head allows me to let go of it, or it to let go of me.

Sometimes you fear a change because you are imagining a worst-case scenario outcome, and you may have blown the situation out of proportion in your mind. For me, this happened when my husband's employer recently announced that they were once again switching our health insurance plan. Each year we seemed to be offered a worse plan for more money, and immediately I began fearing the change. However, when I stopped reacting and actually looked into the change, I was pleasantly surprised that although the plan is new, it is not actually worse. Getting the facts really helped!

Exercise: What is Changing

What changes are occurring in your life and work? Getting these down on paper and out of your head will create a ground of clarity for later actions, if required.

Fear of Public Speaking

The National Institute of Mental Health estimates that 74 percent of us suffer from a fear of public speaking.[25] You don't have to be giving a keynote speech for this fear to kick in. In fact, in work-related situations we are provided numerous opportunities to feel this anxiety, such as when we give presentations, interviews, and performance reviews. These situations are a perfect time to take a pause, and to practice some mindful techniques. When you are preparing yourself for one of these stressful situations, you can give yourself the gift of taking a few deep breaths. Then notice how you can feel the clothes on your skin, the air on your face, and the sounds in the room. Taking these steps, you move out of reactive mode and become grounded in the present moment. This puts you in control, and you can look clearly at the fear, see the story you are telling yourself, and observe how the fear is manifesting in your body. When you look directly at your fear, with the anchor of your breath, you'll feel the storyline begin to dissipate and lessen its hold on you, and you'll be able to move forward with your activity.

Micro-Practice: Using Breath to Deal with Fear

- Stop
- Take a few deep breaths in and out
- Feel the ground beneath your feet, notice how your clothes feel against your skin, feel the air on your body, and listen to any sounds in the room
- Allow yourself to be present and allow your thoughts to lessen their hold on you

---

Management by Fear

It is fairly easy to tap into a person's fear and use it as a motivator. The fear of being judged as a "slacker," of being talked about by others, of unfair criticism, of being excluded from important meetings and decisions, and of not being promoted can spur us to work harder and spend an unreasonable amount of hours at work. Why would a manager cultivate an atmosphere like this? It might be because, from their perspective, it works!

The problem, of course, is that fear as a motivator will provide a short-term payoff but exacts a long-term toll. The consequences of maintaining this kind of negative, pressure-cooker environment are the decline of individual health and performance, and eventually the business itself will suffer because innovation and creativity do not flow in an atmosphere of fear.

There are signs when negative motivators are at play. As a leader you can recognize these warnings, and take responsibility for shifting your work culture away from fear. For instance, if you notice that important feedback is being withheld from you, it may be that people in your organization fear retaliation when truth is shared. How you react to news, particularly bad news, signals another person to either continue talking or stop communicating with you. If you roll your eyes or grimace when a message is given, it can signal that you don't want to hear any more, and you may even be contributing to an atmosphere of fear or panic. To avoid perpetuating negativity in your workplace, you can train yourself to pause, take a deep breath, and not react. If you can respond by thanking the messenger for the information or feedback, you will encourage communication.

If ideas are not shared in meetings, it may reflect a fear of humiliation or a belief that no one is listening or cares about what is offered. Unfortunately, it is easy for someone who has raised an idea to be shut down or ignored. If no one responds to input when it is offered, the embarrassment that follows exposing oneself in that way can cause the speaker and others who witness the embarrassment to withhold their ideas in the future. Leaders who acknowledge each person, and every idea that is raised, make it clear that an open process is valued, and that it's safe for team members to throw their thoughts into the ring. Acknowledgment does not mean that every idea will be accepted, but it does communicate respect for varied opinions.

This is also a place where leading by example can have a big impact. Ideally, the leaders in your organization will be open to exchange in meetings, but if this is not the case, individuals can still make a difference by acknowledging colleagues' ideas and comments when they're offered. This simple act of kindness will help improve your work environment, whether or not you're a leader in your organization.

If you find that resistance and fear arise when a new person is joining your team, it may be that the original team members fear being replaced, or perhaps they are simply dealing with fear of change. In either case, it is helpful to be open and clear about your intentions if you're in a leadership role. Discussing the reasons for a new hire and explaining what you are trying to accomplish can dispel concerns. Including your group by inviting feedback in this discussion can contribute to collaboration and strengthening of the team that originally felt threatened. If you are a team member and your manager has not offered any clarity, you could initiate this conversation and help clear the air about the coming change.

If risks are not taken, and everyone implements only ideas and strategies that have been tried before, it could be that your organization does not allow for failure, or that your colleagues fear punishment for failure. Of course, with no risk-taking, there can be no creativity or innovation. Again, as a leader, you have the opportunity to create an atmosphere where questioning the group logic or suggesting a totally different approach is okay and even encouraged. In an atmosphere where risk is tolerated, not all risky ideas will be brilliant, but some of the ideas proposed will be novel and may lead to creative solutions.

The Neuroscience of Fear

The fear or panic response that is still active in our human biology, and may be triggered at work, originally served an important purpose in the survival of the human race. The part of our brain that assesses danger and regulates emotions is an ancient structure—the amygdala—whose function involves the expression and memory of emotions. One of the amygdala's main functions is to protect us from threat. The amygdala senses danger or challenge and sends out an alarm to the body to be ready for "flight or fight." If you're out hunting and a tiger spots you, for example, your body pours out hormones that stimulate your ability to react and flee quickly! The amygdala is not rational; it broadcasts this message whenever triggered.

These days, most of us do not face threats like tigers, warrior invaders, or someone trying to steal our food supply. However, when we receive a negative e-mail, feel insulted by a colleague, or sense our department budget might be cut, our bodies react to these perceived psychological threats with the same fight-or-flight outpouring of hormones. When these chemicals hit our bodies, our heart begins racing, our muscles prime themselves for action, and we're in reactive mode before the rational part of our being even fully registers the situation.

When your stress level is low to moderate, you are less susceptible to this level of reactivity, and in small doses, the hormone the amygdala releases, cortisol, can wake us up and help us focus. However, when cortisol production is constantly stimulated by high levels of stress in the workplace, the amygdala is triggered to actually shut off our rational thinking, which takes place in the prefrontal cortex (PFC). The PFC is where conscious control and decision making take place.

The fact that the conscious part of our brain actually gets turned off when the fight-or-flight reaction is triggered is another survival mechanism; in an emergency, action needs to be taken "unthinkingly" and immediately in order to protect us from harm. When this impulse causes you to write an angry e-mail and hit send before your rational brain considers the consequences, however, it causes harm rather than protection.

The good news is that we now understand that we can train our brains to be more "emotionally intelligent" and less reactive. Our brains are neuroplastic, which means that *what* we pay attention to actually changes the structure and function of our brain. Mindfulness meditation, where we train our attention to return to our breathing, activates the rational, decision-making part of our brain, our prefrontal cortex. As we practice over time, we strengthen our ability to focus our attention, and the effect is that the brain grows new neural connections between the PFC and the amygdala—in other words, mindfulness meditation actually changes your brain structure. These findings have been substantiated by multiple studies, including some with novice meditators who practiced for short periods of time over only eight weeks.[26] Your fear response can be regulated, and you will enjoy less stress and better focus as a result.

Facing Your Fear

Up to this point, we have been looking at a number of external situations that support a fearful workplace. Ultimately, there is internal work we each can do, regardless of the external situation, that will have a big impact on our ability to lead the way to a healthier workplace. In order to make choices that are counter to habitual patterns that have held us back, we have to face the anxiety and uncertainty that the unknown poses, and believe that we are fundamentally worthy of the outcome we wish for. You have to take this kind of leap of self-empowerment for anything different and meaningful to occur. It requires both effort and courage to walk this path. It is a journey of learning to face fear that can be considered in the following three ways:

FEARLESS LOOKING: Looking honestly at both the shadow and the brilliance within yourself and your situations. This starts with examining your mind, using both your intellect and your sense faculties.

FEARLESS FEELING: Feeling your connection to your world, and developing your emotional intelligence and the courage to be authentic. Feeling engages your heart, emotions, and intuition, and connects you even more deeply with your own body and the world around you.

FEARLESS ACTION: Acting compassionately beyond the conventional bounds of hope and fear, and genuinely becoming a part of the solution to everyday world problems that entangle all our lives. This is the result of your mind/body, intellect/emotions, and personal/ transpersonal synchronicities. Such action is powerful because it flows from your genuine humanity and is not limited by self-interest.

We are all afraid of something, or many things. We are afraid of change, or of things not changing. We are afraid of illness, war, degradation of the ecosystem and economy, and death. Fear itself is not the problem. Fear is actually quite intelligent; it alerts us to pay attention. How we move outward to manifest from that dot of fear—that is the challenge and the test for each of us in every moment of our lives. We live in a society and time that is permeated with fear, and each moment presents an opportunity and choice. We can react, or we can respond.

Some years ago, I read a story about unrelenting fear that is illustrative of this process. A young boy was admitted to a psychiatric hospital for observation because of recurring nightmares that prevented him from staying asleep at night. By the time of his hospitalization, he had seen specialists, taken medication, and tried hypnosis and therapy. Nothing worked, and his health was suffering because of his extreme exhaustion. While waiting to take an MRI scan, he found himself next to another child his age who asked him why he was there at the hospital.

"When I go to sleep at night the same dream happens over and over again," he said. "I am being chased by monsters and no matter how fast I run they are right there behind me, ready to catch me and eat me up."

The other boy said, "That sounds really terrible, but do you know why they are chasing you?"

"No," said the boy.

"Did you ever ask them?" the other child asked.

That night the boy went to sleep and before long he was trapped again in his same nightmare—but this time he stopped running, turned around, and for the very first time looked directly at the monster who was chasing him.

"What do you want?" the boy asked.

The monster answered, "I just want to get to know you."

After that, the boy's nightmares ceased.

This story illustrates how we have the tendency to close down and not look at our own fear. This armoring can prevent us from connecting to what lies beneath our fear. What we cannot touch because we have closed ourselves off is our vast self, where our deepest human qualities abide. When we drop our armor and meet our vast self—that is who we have really wanted to know.

If we want to be happy and at peace with ourselves and others, if we want to give and feel love, if we want our lives to make a difference, we each have to look into our fear and the particular fantasy we have created that numbs us and separates us from our truth. Only then can we awaken and truly connect directly with life. In the workplace, if you want to be free to contribute and express yourself, if you want to make a difference in transforming a culture of fear, you must examine what's constraining you; unless you do that, you can't expect the situation to change.

One of my clients, Nancy, worked for a large mortgage processing firm. The pressure to produce a large number of ready-to-sign contracts each day was enormous, as the margin on each was small. The CEO of the company ruled by fear of termination for even the smallest of infractions. Break times and lunches were very short and strictly enforced. There was absolutely no "downtime" allowed. In the midst of this environment, Nancy, a practitioner of meditation, was a senior manager of a unit producing VA mortgages. She felt the fear, and experienced stress because of it. She was so tense she could hardly sleep, and never felt that she was working hard enough. She almost handed in her resignation several times, but then would spend time in meditation and contemplative practice, examining the situation, and would emerge feeling willing to try a better way to motivate her employees.

Nancy sensed that the atmosphere of micro-managing was actually slowing people down, and sapping both energy and enthusiasm for their work. So she began to loosen the rules in her department. People no longer had to follow a strict schedule of breaks; they could stand, stretch, or have a snack when needed. She also extended her employees' lunchtimes, and made sure to have lunch with some of her department colleagues each day. She built a team of mutual respect in the midst of this fearful culture.

No one in the larger company knew about Nancy's policies, but in time they noticed that her department was the highest producer of contracts, week after week, and they asked her how she accomplished this. They were surprised that the key was her interest in the needs of her employees. It took courage for Nancy to implement those steps in the midst of the prevailing work culture, but she did it, and it had a big impact.

Harnessing Your Fear

Working with fear is very personal for me. In many situations, fear has stopped me and shut me down. When my children were young and I was home with them, I developed a deep interest in art, but I was initially reluctant to follow my passion as a clay artist because fear told me, "Your sister is the artist in the family, don't go there." It happened again when I decided to get an MBA: "You are terrible at math; how will you pass calculus?" fear chided me. After obtaining the degree, I then doubted that I could handle the corporate world, "You hate schedules and rules—you won't succeed there," the voice said. It was relentless.

Nevertheless, I pursued each of these arenas—in spite of, or maybe actually because of, my fears—and I began to realize that each time I could clearly identify something I was afraid to do or try, I had identified a chance to grow.

My inspiration to persevere in the face of fear was strengthened in the aftermath of a terrible car accident I was involved in shortly after I earned my MBA. I broke some cervical vertebrae, and could have easily lost my life or my mobility, but I didn't. As a result, I decided that while I am alive, there is no point in not doing something just because I am afraid!

Life itself is volatile, uncertain, complex, and ambiguous (VUCA), and we don't live forever. That is enough reason for fear to arise. We also have the great opportunity to shape our lives by how we respond to what occurs. Now, years after surviving that accident, I am more aware than ever of the important link between facing fear and the ability to connect with a strength and underlying confidence that is a part of my human nature. This is not a confidence that I have to manufacture, but rather a radiant energy that powers, or "empowers," my life. That connection between facing fear and discovering innate confidence is a key component to leading our lives with more joy, ease, and compassion. The very compassion, or love, that is truly our nature allows us to transform the culture of our lives, if we wish to do so. When we examine our fear and touch our true nature, we also discover the deep and complex connectedness we have to others.

Exercise: What Do You Fear?

Read the following quote from Pema Chodron:

"Fear is a universal experience. Even the smallest insect feels it. We wade into the tidal pools and put our fingers near the soft, open bodies of sea anemones and they close up. Everything spontaneously does that. It's not a terrible thing that we feel fear when faced with the unknown. It is part of being alive, something we all share. We react against the possibility of loneliness, of death, of not having anything to hold on to. Fear is a natural reaction of moving closer to the truth."[27]

(continued on next page)

(continued from previous page)

Before you read further, ask yourself, "What do I fear?" and do some journaling. If you run out of thoughts, just keep writing the question over and over until more comes to you. It is very important to be gentle with yourself as you explore your fears. Allow yourself to go deep and run out of ideas, and allow for new thoughts to arise. Keep asking yourself the question, even when it is uncomfortable. You can also use the following prompts:

- When I think about my work/career, what really scares me is . . .
- When I think about my family and close friends, what really scares me is . . .
- When I think about the bigger issues the human race faces, what really scares me is . . .

No one will see this list but you, and it is most helpful if you are genuinely honest with yourself. If you have had a personal traumatic experience that you don't wish to reawaken, you may want to skip this section.

Your list is personal and contains information important to you. Yet beyond the personal, whatever is on the list represents the manifestation of *life unfolding always somewhat beyond our ability to control it.* We would like to be able to construct a known world, one within which we are omnipotent and competent. But this desire results in us defining our self and our world in a tight and constricted manner. Everything within our stuffy, self-defined world belongs to "me," and everything beyond its border is "other." The good news is that once you look at your list and at your fears, you will be empowered to ask them, "What do you want?" and "What is called for here?" Your fearless looking will allow you to take the next courageous steps: opening to feeling and taking action on what you have discovered. By looking, you have made a first move. If you can allow yourself to look again and again, you can open and soften into your heart, and know if it is the right time for you to face a fear and make a change.

The Courage to Change

"We gain strength, and courage, and confidence by each experience in which we really stop to look fear in the face . . . we must do that which we think we cannot."
—Eleanor Roosevelt

When we live within a self-designed comfort zone of habit, everything else is experienced as a threat, and fear arises. As long as this situation is hidden from our awareness, we can only *react* to what we perceive as a threat. Awareness of our self-styled cocoon brings a breath of fresh air into this stuffy world in which we have been living, and we can begin to see the possibility of making a different choice—of not reacting. When we are reacting, a habitual pattern of behavior usually dictates how we respond. We each have our own set of patterns, which mindfulness practice reveals to us over time. Once we see what our triggers are, and how they set our reaction in motion, we have created the space and opportunity to change. We may even realize that we operate with a different set of behaviors when we are at home or with close friends than when we are at work. It is possible, even likely, that fear is a more constant companion at work than we even realize, and that we don't know how deeply it has been affecting our behavior.

This fear is not our enemy. It is actually a hallmark of intelligence, which reveals a place to look at more deeply. When we are open to the big picture, to the interdependence of all the factors that come together in each instant, it is not illogical that may we want to close down in recognition of our VUCA (volatile, uncertain, complex, and ambiguous) world. That is what fear does. But we have the capacity to stay open, strengthen our cognitive functioning, and reduce the reactivity of the fear impulse, and we can develop that capacity through mindfulness practice. We can utilize these results in any moment by taking a breath and a pause, and allowing even small moments of mindfulness to ventilate our day.

Buddhist meditation master Chogyam Trungpa offers us the phrase "Smile at fear" as an alternative to being ruled by it. He suggests that in practicing mindfulness, and in looking at what closes down our hearts, we are expressing the ultimate courage: that of "not being afraid of who you are."

If we can look directly at our lives, including our work lives, we can begin to experience the challenging scenarios of life in light of the wisdom they hold. This takes genuine courage—courage that starts with that willingness to look more deeply into our own minds and hearts.

Being happy and healthy is a discipline you can engage with. You can train your brain to first recognize your habits, then to break the bad habits and adopt more healthy ones. When you are operating from fear-based habits and beliefs, it is as if you are on a "default" setting. In this amygdala-controlled default mode, you are not responding based on conscious choice. When you begin to recognize your different expressions of fear, you won't have to be under their power.

When we can't control our busy thinking mind, it can lead to a feeling of constant worry. Worrying is a pervasive habit that keeps you occupied, and also can prevent you from putting the little things into perspective. You can recognize and curb your worry by seeing it and developing a sense of humor about how amazingly creative your imagination must be to conjure up those ruminative scenarios. Then you have the choice to stop, breathe, and not react to every concern that pops into your head.

Anxiety is an ever-present, low-grade form of fear. Through mindfulness training, we can recognize certain moments of anxiety as reminders to wake up again and again to what is happening. Because we prefer to feel at ease, we usually try to get rid of those reminders and make our experience smooth and pleasurable. Mindfulness will certainly lessen your anxiety, because it will help you release ruminative and unhelpful thoughts by becoming aware of them—and of course you don't want to live in a perpetual state of anxiety. Yet closing ourselves off to all messages that make us anxious or fearful is not always the courageous choice, and it won't help us express our highest potential and vision. For example, anxiety over not meeting a deadline can be a nudge to ask for assistance on that project. Anxiety about your job security can inspire you to set up an appointment with your boss to discuss how you can further meet the needs of your organization. You can use your anxiety to move forward into action if you act with courage and step out of habit.

In order to take this look under the surface of our habitual behavior, we need the tool of mindfulness, and also the tools of gentleness, openness, and bravery. In the following chapters, we will explore practices that access intuition, open the heart through compassion, and allow us to connect with a bigger unknown. Together, these practices will enable you to harness and go beyond the subtle manifestations of fear that appear in your behavior. And when you are no longer ruled by fear, you will be able to ride the energy that is released.

CHAPTER 4:

Listen and Be Heard

Good communication is essential for a successful and well-functioning workplace, and yet there are so very many ways for it to go wrong! At the root of all communication issues is something personal. For at least one of the individuals involved in noncommunication, there could be any of the following issues standing in the way:

- lack of confidence in you, or in the information you have to share,
- fear of the person you need to contact,
- fundamental lack of interest in anyone except yourself.

When someone feels insecure or undervalued, fearful, or pitted against others for resources, or when they are self-absorbed, they are unlikely to be inspired to share information. In a workplace that more highly rewards individual achievement than collaborative outcomes, there is pressure to withhold information and win at the expense of others. Perhaps this occurs where you work.

Have you ever been waiting for key information in order to finish a project on time, or to give a client some information they requested? It can be extremely frustrating and probably makes you feel that your unresponsive colleague is acting quite unprofessional. If you're working with someone who is withholding information or being an ineffective communicator, consider that it could be because of one of the personal reasons mentioned above. The best thing we can do in these situations is be mindful of the busy schedule of others, and at the same time be very clear and repeat our needs when information is not arriving. Of course, we can also model care for the needs of others by swiftly responding when we are asked for help. These are healthy habits to adopt that will have a positive impact on workflow and increase ease between members of your workgroup.

The foundation of clear and caring communication between individuals is at least as important as making sure that systems and protocols are in place. Establishing that foundation involves taking the initiative to understand how to listen well, how to be clear in our messaging, and how to handle difficult subjects and conversations. Good communication is based on the skills of staying present, being open to divergent opinions, and genuinely having an interest in others. It is an expression of both mindfulness and compassion in action, and can be nurtured with intention and attention. Mindful communication and listening can be a path to greatness, both in yourself and for your company. The free flow and exchange of communication will make for a happier workplace!

Gossip and Rumors

What a waste of time and energy gossip at the workplace is, and yet most offices are plagued by the pervasive activity of talking about others and what we think they are doing. Sometimes it's just idle trash talk; sometimes it's talk of pending layoffs, possible budget cuts, or cutting of certain departments. Whatever the topic, this type of speculative communication can cause great stress and depress morale, and it takes place when leaders aren't transparent. In a vacuum of information, people make things up!

As a leader, you can be a part of the solution by extending trust and being more transparent across the board around issues your employees may need to know—ranging from scheduling to job security and everything in between. When employees understand what's happening, they won't have to speculate.

Gossip, as defined in a 2012 study done by the Georgia Institute of Technology, is "the absence of a third party from the conversation."[28] And this kind of communication flows from person to person, through conversation and through our e-mails. In the study, Georgia Tech researchers looked at over 517,000 e-mails sent by Enron employees prior to its collapse. They determined that more than 14 percent of e-mails sent contained gossip, and that negative gossip was 2.7 times more frequent than positive gossip. Gossip is toxic, and while it alone did not bring Enron down, its prevalence points to the existing cancer within the organism that was this failing company.

In your own company, as an individual, you have the power to break the gossip cycle. Gossipers thrive on attention, and if you change the subject, walk away, or simply do not show interest, you can cut the flow of that conversation. Also, you need to be responsible for not talking about others, and even not gossiping about yourself. Of course, this is not all that easy to do, and you are not a terrible person if you speak about one of your coworkers. What's important is that you become aware of your participation in gossip, and realize that you can choose to change this habit if you wish.

If you are an employer or leader, you must communicate regularly about what is happening in the workplace, officially discourage gossip in company policies, and not participate in it yourself. The Georgia Tech study uncovered the interesting fact that directors and VPs spread gossip both up and down the hierarchy of the company, and that CEOs were among the biggest offenders when it came to sending gossipy e-mails.[29] So leaders and employees alike need to pay attention to this issue and reduce gossip in the workplace.

Micro-Practice: Noticing the Effects of Gossip

Reflect on a recent negative conversation you had with a colleague about someone who was not present for your exchange. How did that make you feel? How did that negativity affect your mood and work performance? Did the negative feelings linger?

Micro-Practice: Am I Gossiping?

Sometimes you may need to bring up another person in a conversation. If you and a colleague find yourself talking about a third person who is not present, here is a simple test to know if you're gossiping: Ask yourself, "Would I be saying this if that person was present with us?" If the answer is no, it is gossip, and you should stop.

Electronic Communication

E-mail and texting are here to stay, and they can be a great help in sharing information quickly and easily. However, e-mails can be missed or lost, and texts don't always make it to their destination. Live follow-up is the best way to make sure your information arrived. On the receiving end, a bigger problem with e-mail is our tendency to read it too quickly, jump to a conclusion, and pound out a reactive response. On more than one occasion, I have regretted not taking another minute to read the letter more carefully and for detail! Mindfulness plays an important role here, as does the emotional regulation that develops from it. If you feel triggered when you receive an e-mail, you can use the STOP technique, which is an extended application of the mindful pause.

Micro-Practice: STOP

Stop—Stop whatever you are doing. You can even say the word to yourself or out loud. This interrupts your reactive mind.

Take a breath—Take a few breaths deep into your belly and out through your mouth. Deep breathing increases the flow of oxygen to the brain and activates the parasympathetic nervous system, which promotes a sense of calmness.

Observe—What are you thinking? Feeling in your body? Feeling emotionally? Observing what you are experiencing has the effect of reducing your fear/reactive response.

Proceed—Mindfully, without reaction, decide how to respond. Re-read the e-mail and check for understanding and details you may have missed.

Sometimes it is best to wait an hour or a day before responding to an e-mail that upsets you.

Rotary International is a service organization whose mission includes encouraging high ethical conduct standards for business and professional leaders. In 1932, they developed a guide to communication conduct that still applies well in our age of social media. Called the Four-Way Test, it asks members to be sure that what they think, do, or say passes this test: Is it true? Is it fair to all concerned? Will it build goodwill and better friendships? Will it be beneficial to all concerned? If we were to use this test to check whether our conversations are gossip or whether we should press send on that e-mail, we would go a long way toward applying mindfulness and compassion to our daily activities—benefiting both work relationships and work flow.

The Power of Curiosity

When we were children, we were taught three basic steps to safely cross a busy street: Stop, look, listen. These same simple instructions bring mindfulness to play in our daily lives. If we can stop, breathe, and become present, we can make room for curiosity to arise. When we are so absorbed with our own rumination on what we did wrong in the past, or with anticipating and worrying about what is coming in the future, it is hard to really look at or listen to what is really happening in front of us, and also within us. The times when we are only listening to our own thoughts are the times when we make a wrong turn, misinterpret what someone has just said, or get hit by a car. However, when we can see what our minds are manufacturing and learn to let go with greater ease into "now," we get lots of important messages from the world, including when it is safe to cross the street.

Your explorations thus far may have begun to reveal to you ways in which you are not totally open to the messages coming toward you. Distortions, personal biases, cultural views, habits, and fear all limit our ability to connect directly with what is happening and what is being communicated. Fortunately, the practice of mindfulness and the resulting awareness of limiting beliefs opens the door to a powerful antidote to these afflictions: curiosity! As Albert Einstein said of his accomplishments, "I have no particular talents, I am only passionately curious."

Curiosity starts with choosing to be present. This increase of awareness is an incremental process that you can notice even as a beginner of mindfulness practice. As you begin to slow down your tumble of thoughts and develop an ability to return to the present moment, you will naturally start to take a greater interest in the details of your life.

One of the places where this enhanced curiosity has the most impact is in your role as a listener. As a genuinely curious listener, you open a space for real exchange, empower the speaker to fully express their views, and create an environment for learning and creativity to spark. When we are curious, we are being inquisitive, free from judgment. We want to learn and understand.

Think about a meeting where a presenter goes on and on about their project or point of view with the sole intention of convincing you that they are right. How does that make you feel? Now imagine a meeting where you are invited to share your thoughts and ideas. It is pretty clear which situation is the one where you close down and don't even hear half of what is being said. As a leader, you have the opportunity to encourage learning and creative solutions in meetings by creating an environment where open exchange takes place.

Exercise: Transforming the Culture of Meetings: Applied Curiosity

Relationships between two or more people are the ground of action and potential change in any situation and/or organization. The following suggestions can help lay the ground for a more open and productive work environment:

- When beginning any meeting, make a clear beginning moment—distinguish the exchange to follow from the random chatter that may have preceded it. You may want to create a spacious pause, with no talking for several seconds until you have everyone's attention.
- A "check-in" of one or two sentences can be a method for getting those present to share their state of mind. If someone in the group needs support, it could be offered, or perhaps they could be excused to deal with a more urgent need, if necessary.
- Now the group present is more grounded and connected to each other, and the meeting can proceed. In some organizations, the next step could be taking a minute for everyone to sit in silence and reflect on issues about to be addressed. This will establish greater presence and focus for the meeting.
- Another possibility is to discuss one of the more contentious items for the meeting in pairs before addressing it as a group. In these dyads, a formal speaker/listener format can be utilized so that each person feels fully heard, and the listeners have a chance to practice mindfulness.

- When a colleague speaks, whether in the larger meeting or dyad, really try to open your mind and heart and hear the other person's point of view. Notice your tendency to be thinking of your answer or argument; notice how you miss what they were saying when you are thinking about yourself.
- This kind of listening practice will eventually result in greater understanding and respect for others, openness to new ideas, and greater collaboration.

Forbes magazine cites curiosity as a source of innovation, and one of the most important skills for today's successful leader. After all, as a leader, if you are not open and curious, you can only take your company down paths that have already been explored. In his article "Steve Jobs and the One Trait All Innovative Leaders Share," author August Turak points out that voracious curiosity early in life greatly affected the careers of Bill Gates, Warren Buffett, and Steve Jobs. He notes, "Jobs wasn't curious because he wanted to be successful, he was successful because he was so curious."[30] This general wide-ranging curiosity is responsible for most scientific discoveries as well. Researchers follow many ideas down their winding paths until, perhaps much to their surprise, the puzzle pieces fall into place one day and a discovery is made. This is the fruit of genuine curiosity, not linear goal orientation.

The Far-Reaching Benefits of Curiosity

Research published in the online Cell Press journal *Neuron* gives us a glimpse of what happens in our brains when our curiosity is aroused. Learning and memory function more efficiently when you have a deep desire to know the answer to something. While that's not a surprising finding, there was another, more unexpected, finding: the effect of a person's aroused curiosity continued on after their initial interest in the subject matter, even when neutral information was presented.[31] This means that if you can engage the curiosity of a colleague, customer, or potential client in the early part of a conversation or presentation, they will stay engaged even when you get to the point of presenting less interesting information. Dr. Matthias Gruber of UC Davis explains it this way: "Curiosity may put the brain in a state that allows it to learn and retain any kind of information, like a vortex that sucks in what you are motivated to learn, and also everything around it."[32] The fact that the mind stays curious and open to information once it's engaged is something we ought to try to integrate into our awareness as we plan our communication of important information. If we present an engaging story at the opening to our presentation, we can expect that our audience's attention will remain engaged even for the "facts and figures."

Researchers looking at brains aroused by curiosity have noted increased activity in the brain circuits connected with reward and the neurochemical dopamine—a chemical messenger that relays between brain circuits and makes us feel good, leading to a sense of relaxation.[33] Our health in general may also be enhanced by our inquiring minds. In a study published in 1996 in *Psychology and Aging*, researchers found that in a pool of more than 1,000 adults aged sixty to sixty-eight, those who were rated as being more curious at the start of the study were more likely to be alive at the end of the study five years later. This was true even after the study considered whether these participants smoked or had cancer or cardiovascular disease![34]

In 2005, another 1,000 patients were the subject of an article in the journal *Health Psychology*. This two-year study reported that individuals with higher levels of curiosity were associated with a lower likelihood for developing diabetes or hypertension.[35] These findings excite me since I'm such voracious reader—so much so that my husband has often joked that I should buy stock in Amazon, since they are delivering books to our home daily. It's great to know that my insatiable curiosity might help me to live a longer and healthier life. These studies also point to the power of work that excites and stimulates to increase everyone's overall well-being.

The most powerful result of a curious mind may well be the enhanced ability to experience things that excite and inspire us. When we are inspired, work can feel meaningful. While not every job has the potential to satisfy our sense of purpose, we can aim to make a greater connection between our self and the work we do. As individuals, the personal assessment of your interests and strengths you performed while reading Chapter 1 of this book can be a trigger for a conversation about engaging in work that inspires you. If you are a leader, you can be open to these conversations, and try to connect workers with their areas of interest. When individuals are truly curious about a subject, they find greater meaning and purpose in pursuing knowledge and excellence around that topic. While intense passion for a subject may not always be possible, when we allow, foster, and encourage curiosity in our workplaces, it can have a profound effect on actual bottom-line results and will greatly enhance the retention of key employees. When work feels meaningful, curiosity arises naturally, and that can lead to more engagement and happiness in the performance of daily tasks.

Exercise: Active Curiosity—Reaping the Benefits of Curiosity Every Day

Move toward uncertainty. Instinctively, you may think that you will be happier if you choose to perform familiar activities. However, we actually derive a more intense and longer-lasting positive experience from trying something new. The discovery and surprise is worth the anxiety and tension that may precede it.

- Challenge yourself by doing something unfamiliar this week. For instance: pick up an instrument you haven't touched in years, or try writing a poem, or take a walk in a neighborhood you have never visited. Notice how you feel and what you are aware of and remember.

Look for the unexpected in the familiar. This is an exercise in suspending your ordinary judgment and peering into what is really happening, rather than your expectation of the situation.

- Choose an ordinary "boring" activity you have to perform each day, such as filing the papers on your desk or creating a to-do list for the next day. As you do it, see if you can notice three aspects of that task that you have not noticed before. For example, you might notice the satisfaction you get from feeling organized, or the sense of space you gain from sorting and filing the papers on your desk.

Try something entirely new. Challenge yourself to learn something you have previously not been interested in. See what you notice about that activity.

- Try a yoga class; try singing; put on some roller blades (and protective gear!)—you get the idea!

Get curious about yourself. What excites your passions? What did you use to love that is no longer part of your world? What do you feel called to do that is not a part of your day?
- Consider adding an activity to your life that reconnects you with your personal passion.

Relax, Be Gentle, and Let More In

Listening well is a gift we give not only to ourselves but also to others. Who doesn't cherish the feeling of being heard and understood? From our first cry in this world, we are asking for understanding and for our needs to be met. This never really changes. Partners, children, customers, employees, vendors, clients, colleagues, and shareholders all want their voices heard. Learning to listen mindfully can literally change our lives and livelihoods. There is so much that others are trying to share which would increase our ability to function effectively, yet so often we are caught in hearing only what we expect. If you give your full attention to a client, colleague or competitor, you may well learn what you need to make wiser decisions.

Listening is an active, mindful practice. We choose to place our attention on the other person, and we notice when we have wandered from listening and return to it. Good listening skills will improve communication and relationships, particularly important in complex business situations. Giving your full attention to an employee (or friend, spouse, or child) builds trust and demonstrates that the relationship is valued. It may be helpful to close the door or move to a quiet place to have a mindful conversation, which is a further demonstration of your true interest in what the person will have to say. Although this step might take an extra minute or two, reduced misunderstanding resulting from genuine listening helps improve clarity about and focus on the task to be accomplished, and so may also result in fewer mistakes being made—which ultimately translates to more time.

An additional benefit of you becoming a better listener is that your way of being can have a powerful ripple effect on the people who come in contact with you. The positive feelings that others feel when they are heard may inspire them to become a better listener themselves.

Micro-Practice: Mindful Listening

Practice this during your next important conversation. Try to find a place where you can have an undisturbed exchange. Invite the other person to speak, and don't interrupt them at all. Wait until they finish speaking before you say anything. Open yourself fully to listening with all of your senses. If you notice your mind wandering to form an answer or rebuttal, just notice, as in meditation practice, and return to listening the way you would return to your breath. This is a wonderful application of mindfulness that can enhance all of your communications. It can also serve as a model for others, who will appreciate how well you are paying attention to them.

Listening doesn't happen only with our ears. Any artist who works with visual arts knows that the artwork itself speaks and needs to be heard. I build fountains and other large structures by hand from clay. When I start to create a piece, I have a sketch. I start with a clear idea. That is necessary to begin. However, I know from experience that once I begin to build the piece, the clay will actually tell me what to do. It depends on many factors beyond my control—how the clay body was mixed, how humid or dry the outside conditions are, how thick or thin I roll the clay, how much water I add during the creation process, and how quickly I try to build. Some of my most treasured pieces have taken shape as the result of the interaction and flow between the material and my intentions. Similarly, we get messages all the time from situations, and each other, that can help us to be more flexible and move in a direction that differs from our original intention.

Leaders who inspire loyalty and trust in their employees also go beyond listening with their ears. They are noticing nonverbal cues such as facial expression, demeanor, mood, and work performance. They demonstrate their genuine care for the other person by taking the time to have a conversation that allows important information to be exchanged. It can be hard to listen without judgment when someone else won't look us in the eyes or is checking their phone during a conversation. This calls for the self-awareness arising from mindfulness that allows us to see our own triggers, let them go, and return attention to the other person. Particularly in times of professional and personal challenges, employees want leaders who care about their general well-being, not just their work output. This listening comes not only from the head but also from the heart. You could say that this is an expression of gentleness or compassion in addition to mindfulness in action. A leader who has the confidence to express empathy and not be afraid of displays of stress or of sentiment is expressing key components of emotional intelligence—the ability to perceive, understand, and manage emotions. We will discuss this important personal and interpersonal skill, which derives from mindfulness, further in Chapters 6 and 7.

Intuition and Decision-Making

There are messages and activities going on in the world just beneath the surface of what you notice. By paying attention to details, you may find answers you never expected and connections you had not anticipated, and notice opportunities you might have missed. You will feel a confidence in your decision-making, and a peace of mind that comes from noticing what is available and knowable.

Intuition as a topic of interest is popular now in business, as evidenced by the number of blog posts and news articles on sales intuition, business intuition, and strategic intuition. For instance, I recently read that the success of Coco Chanel was not due only to her hard work, ambition, and sense of style but also to her trusting her intuition. She sensed what women wanted, and then created demand for it. The merits of trusting intuition have also been touted by business luminaries like Bill Gates and Warren Buffett—who, incidentally, have been noted as being highly curious individuals as well. Being curious and trusting our intuition are not unrelated. Oprah Winfrey, whose whole business model is based on sharing the fruits of her curiosity, has the following business advice: "Follow your instincts. That's where true wisdom manifests itself." Nevertheless, many people still discount the role that intuition can serve in business and in life. In our complex and information-oversaturated world, it is often difficult to reach a clear decision through analysis alone. Now more than ever it is more important to reconsider a bias against intuition, and open to include our internal wisdom.

Years ago, I actually saved my own life by trusting an instinctive thought. I was about to give birth to my second child; my first delivery had been by C-section, and the doctors, who were being pressured by insurance companies to cut down on the number of these operations they performed, told me we would try for a natural delivery this time. While I had no problem with this decision, I asked, "What are the reasons for not having a vaginal birth after cesarean?"

"In about 5 percent of cases, there can be a rupture resulting in death," the doctor said.

Without a second's hesitation I heard myself say, "That will happen to me. I will die if I have a VBAC."

The doctor looked at me, appalled. "I am going to write down that you are requesting a C-section," he said, "and it probably won't be covered by insurance."

I held to my decision; I was completely certain that I was making the right choice. When my delivery time came, an extremely rare complication was present, and I heard the doctor say to the nurse, "If she were already in labor right now she would have bled to death."

I know this story is graphic, but it illustrates how wisdom arises within us, and how, if we push it away, there can be very serious consequences.

None of our decisions are actually made by intellect alone. In fact, "gut feelings," or emotions, always play a critical role in decision-making. Much of the research in this arena has been done by Antonio Demasio, professor of neuroscience at the University of Southern California. In a popular YouTube video, Daniel Goleman tells the story of one of Demasio's patients who had surgery for a brain tumor. The surgery was successful in that the tumor was removed, but a surgical error was committed in the process: the connection between the amygdala (the emotional brain) and the prefrontal cortex (thinking brain) was snipped. Following the surgery, the patient was able to reason, but he could not make decisions. He was missing the link to his emotional memories.[36] Demasio gleaned from this patient's case, and from others he's treated, that most of what we extract as wisdom in our lives is based on what we learned from our emotional responses. These memories live in our bodily awareness, not our thinking mind.

Let's consider why intuition is so important for you at work. Business is transforming at an accelerated rate, and so is the amount of information we try to digest. A recent UCLA study revealed that we process more than five times the information daily than we did twenty years ago![37] We need to utilize our inherent ability to relate to information at a speed faster than thought processing. This is a skill we all possess that can be further developed through the practice of applying self-awareness to body and emotional awareness.

We call our intuition a "gut feeling," or a "hunch," because it is more connected to what we feel in the pit of our stomach than our mind. In Finland, studies involving 700 participants of different nationalities produced a colorful graphic map representing where every emotion can be felt in our body. The participants in these studies were given two blank human silhouettes. They were then shown a variety of images, ranging from facial expressions to movies to stories and emotional words, and were asked to color the body regions in the silhouettes where they felt the physical sensations of fourteen predetermined emotions while looking at those images. When the results were compiled, there was emotional agreement across all nationalities as to where we feel our emotions in our body.[38] In other words, how we feel emotions is a very human, shared experience that we can learn to notice. By using mindfulness to pay attention to our bodies, we can become more aware of, and familiar with, how we personally experience emotions and intuitions, and how they inform our thoughts and decisions.

In his book *Blink: The Power of Thinking Without Thinking*, Malcolm Gladwell describes a fascinating study done at the University of Iowa: a gambling experiment intended to demonstrate how we register emotions in our bodies, and how those emotions subconsciously affect behavior and decision-making even before we have cognitive awareness. In the experiment, the players were each given four decks of cards, two red and two blue. Each card turned over from any deck either cost or benefited the players money, depending on the value of the card. Each player was allowed to turn over a total of one hundred cards, with the objective of maximizing winnings. Of course, at the start of the game, the players had no idea that in reality, only the blue decks would average out to be "winning decks." The experiment looked at how long it would take the players to figure this out.

During the experiment, participants were hooked up to a monitor that gauged anxiety by measuring the sweat on their palms. After fifty cards, the participants expressed a "feeling" that two of the decks were better than the others. Only after eighty cards were drawn were the participants able to explain that the two red decks were worse than the two blue decks. Yet at as early as between ten to thirty cards, participants would sweat more when reaching for a card from a "bad" deck, and they began to pick more from the good decks, even though they did not express any knowledge of what their body was telling them or that they were shifting their behavior.[39]

The conclusion from this study is that we are capable of having emotional responses that change our behavior even before we are conscious of them. These responses are felt in our bodies before our cognition processes a situation. Therefore, learning to tune into our bodies and emotions, learning to trust our "hunches," can be an important advantage when it comes to making the quick decisions required by our fast-paced times.

We often second-guess ourselves when we have an intuitive feeling. Can you think of a time when you knew to do something but you overrode your instinct? It is helpful to look at your own relationship to intuition in order to learn how you sense knowledge from the inside out. You need to see the patterns of when your feelings are correct and helpful, and when they may be colored by prior experiences. Intuition should be relied upon in conjunction with knowledge, research, and good information. It does not exist in isolation; rather, it is another powerful sense we can call upon in our uncertain times.

The following exercise will help you make a connection to feelings your own body, including internal sensations, where we experience intuition. So much of the time we live in our heads and don't relate to what we are feeling. By doing this exercise from time to time, you will strengthen the neural connections in your insula, the area of the brain that integrates and processes sensory information with cognitive thinking. This exercise will also help you to notice and lessen your emotional reactivity.

Exercise: Body Scan—An Exercise for Deepening Intuitive Sensing

A body scan can help us to develop emotional awareness and allow us to tune into parts of our own bodies we may habitually ignore. When we can feel, we can receive the messages our body is transmitting. This type of mindful check-in can be done anytime and anywhere. When you feel you need a mental break at your desk, you can take a few minutes to refocus your energy with this simple exercise.

Instructions:

- Stand, sit, or lie down in a comfortable position, making sure that you do not have any constriction. Loosen any tight clothing. Let go of any current concerns, regrets of the past, hopes for the future. Try to bring your attention fully to this moment and take a deep breath to relax.
- Starting with your feet, pay attention to the physical feelings in them: any pain, discomfort, coolness, warmth, tension, tightness, whatever arises. Simply pay attention to the physical feelings and sensations.
- Don't judge them as good or bad, don't try to change them, just be aware of them.
- Slowly allow your awareness to travel from your feet to your lower legs, simply paying attention to any physical sensations in that part of your body, including any tightness, pain, or discomfort.
- Then slowly allow your awareness to travel farther up your body, doing the same gentle noticing for all of the parts of your body—your upper legs, hips, buttocks, pelvic region, stomach, chest; your lower back, upper back; your fingers and hands; your lower arms, upper arms, shoulders, neck; your head, forehead, temples; your eyes, cheeks, nose, mouth, jaw line.

(continued on next page)

(continued from previous page)

- Then let your awareness travel gently and slowly back down your body, noticing any other places where there is pain, discomfort, tension, or ease until your awareness settles back at your feet.
- You can begin by doing this exercise for just five minutes. Over time, you can stop worrying about how long it takes, and simply allow yourself to pay attention to the sensations in your body.
- If, while doing this exercise, you find that you have wandered into thinking about something, that's okay. Just notice the thoughts, and then notice yourself noticing the thoughts, and gently guide your awareness back to your body.

When you are grounded in your body, you can notice your thoughts and emotions in an atmosphere of greater space, and not be as caught in your habitual reactions. When faced with a difficult situation, you can tune into what you are feeling in your body and stay open to not reacting in a way that creates further separation. Your lack of reactivity may actually shift the dynamic toward resolution rather than escalation.

We'll explore further keys to staying grounded and open in the face of challenge in the next chapter. A great first step is learning to extend to yourself the warmth, curiosity, and care that you would like to be met with when interacting with others. Everyone deserves this, you first and foremost. Self-care leads to care and communication with others in a wonderful cascade of good will.

CHAPTER 5:

Be Kind to Yourself

In this chapter we arrive at an important turning point. Up to now, the practices of mindfulness we've discussed, both formal and on the job, have been focused on reducing your stress, improving your mental and emotional health, and enhancing communication. The opening of your heart has been a bonus resulting from becoming more aware of yourself and others. In this chapter, I'm going to be urging you to take the heart-opening step of being more actively kind to yourself through the practice of self-compassion. Practicing self-compassion offers an even greater opportunity for personal transformation and leadership authenticity. This step can be pivotal in transitioning from being overwhelmed by the problems we face to becoming an important part of the solution.

The term compassion, without the prefix of "self," actually refers to the impulse to respond to the suffering of *others* by wanting to help. This natural opening of our hearts to others is a powerful source of happiness, and we will soon explore how it works. However, unless we come face-to-face with our own pain and suffering, it's difficult to open our hearts to others. Therefore, working with self-compassion is a necessary place to start. When we are judging ourselves, feeling a lack of self-esteem, or being held back by feelings of fear, taking the time to understand where we are and to hold our own self in kindness can result in a huge shift in our ability to heal our own pain and extend our care to others.

Values And The Seven Levels Of Personal Consciousness

One way to understand how some of our beliefs or values may be limiting us, and the role that self-compassion plays in allowing us to grow beyond our limiting views, is to look at Richard Barrett's model called "The Seven Levels of Consciousness." In my work with clients, I ask them to assess their values on this scale, which Barrett adapted from the Maslow hierarchy, a psychological theory of human needs and motivation developed in 1943. This model can be applied to individuals or organizations, and illustrates how we move from foundational values that concern the self to values that benefit others, an expansion in awareness that mirrors the opening of our hearts to others.

Barrett—along with consultants who use his approach, such as myself—has helped individuals and organizations measure, manage, and upgrade their organizational culture. In Chapter 1, I provided a link to the Barrett Personal Values Assessment (PVA), which returns to you a full report describing these seven levels and where your most important values fall on this scale.[40] If you haven't taken this simple and fun quiz yet, please do so when you are ready.

BARRETT SEVEN LEVELS OF CONSCIOUSNESS

PERSONAL

Service / Selfless Service
widsom, global peace, human rights, humility, compassion, forgiveness, legacy, ethics, vision, global or societal perspective

Making a Difference / Collaboration & Partnerships
coaching, mentoring, leadership development, strategic alliances, environmental awareness, community involvement, employee fulfilment, intuition, empathy, highly inclusive

Alignment, Authenticity
trust, honesty, commitment, enthusiasm, creativity, alignment of values and/or mission, fun

Learning & Continuous Improvement
growth, courage, risk taking, knowledge, balance (work/home), builds consensus, empowers staff, initiative, accountability

Self Esteem & Performance
success, strategy, excellence, quality, productivity, strong analytic, values success, professional growth, skill development, reliability, accuracy, **power, recognition, authority**

Relationships & Connectivity
Values relationships, family, friends, loyalty, respect, tradition, recognition, communication, **demanding, being liked**

Foundations for Survival
health, financial stability, safety, good in crisis, strong financial managers, promote compliance, **job insecurity, caution, authoritarian**

ORGANIZATIONAL

Service to Humanity and the Planet
social responsibility, future generations, long-term perspective, ethics, compassion, humility, sustainability

Strategic Alliances and Partnerships
environmental awareness, community involvement, employee fulfilment, coaching/mentoring

Building Internal Community
shared values, vision, commitment, integrity, trust, passion, creativity, openness, transparency

Continuous Renewal and Learning
accountability, adaptability, empowerment, teamwork, goals orientation, personal growth

High Performance
systems, processes, quality, best practices, pride in performance, **bureaucracy, complacency**

Employee Recognition
loyalty, open communication, customer satisfaction, friendship, employee recognition, and fairness, **manipulation, blame, internal competition**

Financial Stability
shareholder value, organizational growth, employee health, safety, **control, corruption, greed**

7
6
5
4
3
2
1

Once you have your results, you will have an analysis and a visual report of where your values fall on this scale. This powerful assessment can reveal what motivates you, and sometimes the fears that accompany those motivations. It illuminates where you put most emphasis and also where you shy away from taking interest. When you look at your own Personal Value Assessment, it is possible that your chosen values seem "lopsided," falling all at the top or maybe the bottom of the chart. If this is the case and you are part of a larger organization, it will help you to see what functional areas you may need support with.

Recently, I was meeting with the extremely capable CEO of a technical company. When issues having to do with finances came up, she repeatedly said that she would get back to me because she could not make those decisions without talking with key people on her team. When I got back to my office, I took a look at her Personal Value Assessment and realized that every one of the areas that she personally valued were in Levels 4 and above. Intelligently, she has put together a support team that values fiscal responsibility and the foundational values that are not of interest to her. That balance allows her company to thrive.

On the individual level, we can also use this information about what we value most highly to strengthen the areas where we initially have not placed emphasis. When I first took this assessment, I also had several values in the top of the pyramid, expressing a desire to be of service and help make a difference in the world. Yet I did not actually place enough importance on the financial stability that would be necessary to make this value possible. Seeing my own chart and realizing that the grounding values weren't in place helped me realize that I needed to pay more attention to the first level in order to achieve my vision. Over time, I was able to establish this important basis.

With the foundational values in place, it is easier to move outward from self-concern to seeing the bigger possibilities. Barrett's model can be seen as a map to the happier and more productive workplace that we have been examining. It is a visual representation of our journey toward becoming more compassionate and responsive to the suffering in ourselves, our workplaces, and our world.

Hierarchy of Values

In this Consciousness Pyramid, there are three distinct sections. At the base of this pyramid chart are the foundational blocks where we hold values that are either healthy or potentially limiting. To the sides of each of the seven numbered levels, there are descriptions of the values falling in that level of consciousness. Those values which are boldfaced at the end of each of the lower three levels are examples of potentially limiting values..

These first three levels can be thought of as the ground or "earth" levels. Without adequate grounding in the practicalities of financial stability, the connection of interpersonal relationships, and healthy self-esteem, we cannot move on to the transitional level. The first of the three levels can be seen as the ground of our personal or organizational value system. If you have chosen no values in one or more of these levels, it may indicate that you are not putting enough value on basics such as financial stability, friendship, or your own worth. Alternatively, an absence of values in those levels may indicate that you have them so fully integrated that you did not choose to emphasize one or more of those levels. This is an opportunity for contemplation and arriving at a personal interpretation of your assessment. When these assessments are used in organizations, the answers provide a similar map, opening the conversation to where improvements in organizational systems are needed.

Level Four is a transitional level. It represents value for transformation, and the focus here is on awareness and letting go of our fears. Some values that fall in this level could be continuous learning, independence, and personal growth. This is a level that prepares us to open our heart. It is where the practice of self-compassion naturally resides. In an organization, values at this level may additionally look like adaptability, team building, and empowerment of others.

If you have the solid ground of the first three levels, along with awareness of the need to move beyond your fears at Level Four, your values might rise into the upper triangle's three levels of awareness, which are connected to the common good. We can think of these as the more visionary values associated with finding meaning in life. In Level Five we are dealing with self-actualizing and values such as clarity, creativity, and enthusiasm. Level Six moves into making a positive difference in the world, where we might find we value mentoring others. In Level Seven, the level of selfless service to others and "servant leadership," we find values such as vision and wisdom. We will be discussing these qualities in Chapters 6, 7, and 8.

No matter what our values are, or how awake our organizational culture is, the mindfulness practices we have been examining have tangible benefits. They can reduce our stress, center our attention, and improve our communication in difficult situations—and difficult situations will always arise. Self-reliance and high performance can improve when we trust our own intelligence and intuition. A positive self-image is enhanced through reducing reactivity, genuinely engaging with others, and developing self-discipline.

If you're in a place where these issues are still a daily struggle, it can be helpful to see this as a roadmap to personal and organizational growth. As we continue to apply the practices in this and the following chapters, you will see how it is possible—and optimal—to operate with values at all levels of consciousness integrated. You can have financial stability, harmonious relationships, continual growth, a meaningful job, and make a difference in the lives of others, all in the same workplace. Wouldn't that be great? We are getting there, step by step.

Right now we are going to take a step into the realm of transformation, where you will deepen the skills of balance and resilience through the practices of self-compassion and loving kindness. In doing so, you will grow to honor yourself even further. There is a clear correlation between increased happiness and the practices of compassion; so rest assured that by opening your heart you are embarking on a courageous journey toward a happier life and workplace.

Practicing Self-Compassion and Loving Kindness

How do you care for yourself when you feel like your life is in overdrive or out of control? This is a key question, because how you honor and love yourself in the midst of anxiety and challenges will have a big impact on how you communicate, handle difficulty, bounce back from adversity, and inspire action. Think about how we use the word "heart" in everyday language and you will see how our vocabulary expresses its central importance in our life. We say things like, "Let's get to the heart of the matter," or, "My heart tells me not to do that." When you feel moved by something, you might say, "My heart opened." These expressions convey our fundamental heart connection to situations we experience. This connection is real and direct, not confused by second thoughts or judgment.

It can be quite healing to move from head to heart when you are feeling stressed, afraid, critical, or judgmental about work you have produced, a decision you need to make, a conversation that turned out badly, or the way you reacted in a situation. When we feel bad, we often shut down our hearts and replay a situation in our heads, wishing we could have acted differently or that it had played out another way. Focusing on failure in that way can create a self-fulfilling prophecy. When you are self-critical, you may give up when challenges or obstacles arise. This is the choice some of us may make because it saves us from actually having to fail and then being even more critical of ourselves. Also, anxiety about failure can cause us to make poor decisions. As we saw in Chapter 2, when we discussed the role of the amygdala and the freeze, flight, or fight response to fear, when that automatic protective reaction kicks in, our critical thinking is compromised.

An alternative approach when becoming aware of our own fear could be to move into a bigger space of self-acceptance, to open our vast mind and heart and be kind to our self. In the spiritual tradition of Shambhala, we have an expression: "Put that fearful mind into a cradle of loving-kindness." This is a beautiful phrase that points to what we can do to shift out of negative energy states, and also how we can create conditions that help others to move from anxiety to acceptance and presence. When you are in reactive mode, the heart-opening practice of self-compassion can help you to connect with your anxious or difficult feelings in a gentle way that allows you to move in a new direction. The practice of self-compassion is a powerful tool for emotional health at work.

Self-compassion begins with mindfulness: becoming aware of what you are feeling or how you may be judging or criticizing yourself. As you become more familiar with your own self-critical patterns, you can begin to make the choice to be a friend to yourself, to extend kindness to yourself. The compassion practice included in this section will give you a chance to resonate with an unconditional goodness that is always available, that is the essence of who you are as a human being. Through mindfulness practice you experience how to simply be without having to change or prove anything. Just being with situations as they are, without judging or distracting ourselves, can lead to a deeper connection to the truth our feelings reveal. Opening our hearts and accepting our own feelings allows us to relax and reveals the possibility of working with situations we previously may have felt closed off from. Beyond that, softening to our self is an important step toward genuine empathy and compassion for others. Tuning into our hearts in this way allows us have a greater perspective, and actually helps our thinking mind to make better decisions.

Practice: Compassion for Yourself

- Take a comfortable and relaxed posture, and take a few deep breaths in and out. For a few minutes, just focus on your breathing. Feel your body breathing in and breathing out.
- Become aware of what you are feeling in this moment.
- Now, to open your heart, think about someone toward whom you feel a great deal of love. Notice how this love feels in your heart. Notice the sensations around your heart.
- Continue breathing as you think about your loved one, and send them love, care, and wishes for their happiness and well-being. Feel the love radiating from your heart.

(continued on next page)

(continued from previous page)

- Now allow this feeling of love to extend to wishing yourself well. You deserve this love. Give yourself the warmth you shared so freely with your loved one. How does this feel? If it is difficult, send yourself love and appreciation for undertaking this experiment.
- Now bring to mind a time of your own suffering. Maybe a recent time when you were highly self-critical. Perhaps you feel badly about an unresolved work conflict, or about not succeeding at a task that was asked of you.
- Notice how you are feeling as you think of your suffering. Connect with your body, your heart. Can you allow yourself to soften a little further?
- Allow yourself to wish for your suffering to end, for yourself to experience ease and happiness.
- As you breathe, visualize a golden sun in your heart radiating light that eases your suffering. With each exhalation, feel the light rays emanating within you, along with your strong, heartfelt wish that you be free from suffering.
- Silently recite to yourself:

  May I be free from this suffering.
  May I have joy and happiness.

- Repeat this phrase ten times.
- Notice how you are feeling, and give yourself appreciation for taking this time to be self-nurturing.
- Return your attention to feeling your body breathing, open your eyes, and enjoy the moment.

Many people find it much more difficult to generate love for themselves than they do feeling love for others. That is why this exercise begins with generating love for someone that you care about, which opens you up to your own inherent tenderness and capacity for love and compassion. Over time, if you choose to practice self-compassion regularly, it will become easier to feel worthy of this self-care.

Scientific Reasons to Practice Loving Kindness

Dr. Kristen Neff is a leader in the field self-compassion research, which she became interested in after she began her own meditation practice in the 1990s. She decided to put a scientific lens on loving-kindness practices from the Buddhist tradition, which had never before been researched analytically. Her research shows that people who can extend warmth and kindness to themselves are better able to overcome their anxiety and stress, and are much more likely to be optimistic, happy, and resilient. Her research also indicates that when we take care of ourselves in a compassionate way, we are actually triggering the release of higher levels of oxytocin, the hormone that is activated by interactions between a mother and her child, or receiving or giving a caress.[41] In other words, our body does not differentiate between compassion directed toward self or someone else; both actions elicit the same warm feeling. The recognition and practice of self-compassion, therefore, can be life-changing. We have the power to alter our own emotional state with a gesture of kindness to ourselves!

This release of oxytocin can change our body chemistry, and is especially powerful for those who may have worn themselves down with excessive self-criticism. A high level of self-criticism results in stress, activating our amygdala and the release of cortisol. Neff discovered in her research that people who get to an agitated state as a result of being hard on themselves were able to soothe themselves through touch, and that this was more effective than the usual advice we hear about stopping to take a deep breath when we feel upset. If you are feeling tense or upset, you can give yourself a hug or gently stroke your own arm or face. The physical touch that you give yourself will actually release oxytocin and calm you in the same way that a baby is soothed by being taken in its mother's arms.[42]

Honoring Your Worth

Another important step in creating conditions for happiness in your workplace is to move beyond self-compassion to truly honoring your worth. Your worth is not exactly the same as self-esteem. Your worth is not based on what you accomplish or don't accomplish, but rather on knowing your inherent goodness. What is inherent goodness? It is your shared humanity and your vast self—the self beyond your ego. You access it by staying with what is happening, staying with your heart, and not escaping into mental realms of fantasy, busyness, or avoidance. You also touch it by facing your self-doubt and soothing it with kindness.

The idea that we human beings are inherently good is one that many ancient philosophers examined and taught. Confucius, the influential Chinese philosopher, teacher, and political figure born 551 BC, believed that we know our own goodness and inherently know how to honor our worth. In his Golden Rule, he taught, "Do not do to others what you do not want done to yourself." Mencius, another influential Chinese philosopher-sage born 372 BC, suggested that we are born with goodness but lose track of it due to the pressures of society. Two of his most famous quotes are: "He who exerts his mind to the utmost knows his nature" and "The way of learning is none other than finding the lost mind." The lost mind he refers to is the vast mind we have been exploring how to reconnect with. The current Dalai Lama says, "Basic human nature is compassionate and gentle. On that level, the seven billion human beings are the same. We are all brothers and sisters."[43]

Self-worth comes from knowing fundamentally that you are enough as you are. Life is not perfect, you are not perfect, and if you can accept that, what a relief each day brings!

Why is self-awareness and self-acceptance important for a happier workplace? Because when you can know yourself in this unconditional way, not struggling to be a different you but open to knowing your true self, you show up with self-confidence. You are calm and loving, not only toward yourself but also toward others. You exude authenticity and are attractive in a way that inspires others to honor themselves. This is an important leadership trait, and at its core it involves being comfortable in your own skin. When you honor your own worth, you won't need the approval of others to feel validated.

Ralph Waldo Emerson wrote in his famous essay "Self-Reliance" that to trust your own thought and what is true for you is your genius. The beauty of this inner knowing is that, far from leading to an inflated view of oneself, it leads to seeing goodness in others and recognizing that their genius is innate in them as well. This level of trust in the goodness of ourselves and others is the basis for an expanding circle of respect, interest, and collegiality that will help everyone to succeed.

Micro-Practice:
Honoring Your Goodness

Whenever you think of it, and especially if you are having a moment of hesitation:

- Pause
- Put your hand over your heart (if you are in a safe place to do so)
- Repeat to yourself, "I am basically good. I am basically kind. I am basically wise. I am basically strong."
- Allow yourself to feel the truth of these simple and powerful words.
- Go back to your activity with a greater awareness of your innate worthiness.

The Happiness Connection

Now it is time for the tale of "the happiest man on earth," Matthieu Ricard. Actually, Matthieu doesn't really care for that label, but it accurately describes what scientists discovered about the brain of this extraordinary man. A French genetic scientist turned Buddhist monk (also a photographer and author), Ricard was a volunteer in a study about happiness conducted at the University of Wisconsin at Madison in the lab of Dr. Richard Davidson in 2008. This study was part of a larger body of research done on the brains of hundreds of advanced practitioners of meditation. Ricard is a "master practitioner" of meditation who spent decades in long-term retreat, and the scan of his brain showed two amazing results regarding his meditation practice. First, it showed the highest level of gamma waves—a brain frequency linked to consciousness, memory, attention, and learning—ever recorded. Second, it showed tremendous amount of activity in the left prefrontal cortex (PFC) compared to the right. (The prefrontal cortex, as we discussed in an earlier chapter, is the more recently evolved part of our brain, regulates the emotional reactivity of our amygdala, and can be strengthened as a result of mindfulness meditation practice. Concentrated activity in the left side has been correlated with a larger propensity for happiness and a reduced propensity toward negativity.)

In a TED talk Ricard gave called "The Habits of Happiness," he commented on this study, explaining that the research focused on the brain's neuroplasticity, its ability to grow new neural connections.[44] Davidson was looking at whether the brain could change its normal emotional "set point," or level of joy and happiness, as a result of tens of thousands of hours of meditation practice on loving-kindness as practiced by monks in long-term retreat.

Ordinary individuals (people who had not meditated in retreat over a long period of time) served as control subjects for this study. They were asked to open themselves to unconditional compassion while their brains were being scanned in the same manner as the monks. What resulted was an average range of activity measured between the right and left PFC, with some showing more activity on the left side and others more on the right. People who had more activity in the right PFC were more prone to sadness, anxiety, and worry, while those with more activity in the left PFC tended toward compassionate behavior, happiness, curiosity, and other positive mental states.

The non-meditators' scans revealed their individual basic "set point," or disposition to be either left PFC-tending, more optimistic and happy, or right PFC-tending, more pessimistic and sad. Yet, although they, and all of us, may have a basic habitual tendency to be optimistic or pessimistic, our brains are "plastic" and respond to what we are focusing on. If you are enjoying yourself, the activity in your PFC will shift temporarily more to the left. If you are stressed and angry, more activity will be measured in the right PFC. The fact that Ricard's brain had a stable reading of the most activity in the left PFC ever recorded means that he has a great capacity for happiness and joy. This result was attributed to his meditation practice—and gave him "the happiest man on earth" moniker.

Ricard and his colleagues were expert-level meditators, but the good news is that more recent research, discussed in Melissa Dhal's article in the April 2016 issue of *New York Magazine*, shows that we don't have to be long-term "master meditators" to affect our own happiness.[45] In fact, just by being mindful and aware of your thoughts when you are suffering and then showing yourself understanding and kindness, you can make a difference in your mood.

There are many factors that could explain this. First of all, when you are mindful and aware of a situation, you can see more clearly that just because something failed or did not go as you had hoped does not make *you* a failure. You see the bigger context in which the disappointment occurred, and you don't have to over-identify with the experience. In fact, you can even use failure as a learning opportunity when you achieve this sense of separation between yourself and the event. When you realize that any given situation is not all about you, and that you are part of a bigger picture, you are also more able to experience an inherent connection to others. This feeling of interconnectedness leads to a sense of well-being that can help you experience failures as a normal part of life. The fact that you can influence your happiness through practicing kindness points to why your efforts to be kinder and more compassionate with yourself will have a ripple effect at work.

Micro-Practice: Leaning into Happiness

If you are feeling down, disappointed, or even angry with yourself, take a moment to run through a reset of your emotional set-point by following these simple steps:

1. Be Mindful

Pause and take a few deep breaths. Bring your awareness to what you are feeling. If it helps, you can touch your belly or heart to get more in touch with your feelings. Acknowledge to yourself what you are feeling.

2. Remember You Are Human

Look at the bigger picture of your situation. Bring to mind the fact that this is a shared human experience. You are not alone. Think of someone you can share your experience with who will be supportive and understand your situation. Realize that this is part of being human.

3. Hold Your Feelings in the Cradle of Loving-Kindness

Put your feelings in a cradle of kindness. Send yourself all the love you would give a friend in a similar situation. If you have another moment, add the practice of "Honoring Your Goodness," located earlier in this chapter.

As a "serial entrepreneur" and someone who has had lots of "amazing ideas" (my own opinion, of course)—some of which I have tried out in the world—I can offer the example of experiencing my business forays in one light and finding out that some in my family do not see it the same way! A few years ago, I was enthusing to one of my sisters about my latest passion and "world-changing idea" when she remarked rather harshly, "Oh, not another doomed venture." I was actually shocked. I had no idea she measured the various projects that I had conceived and executed by whether or not they had lasted or made tons of money. Her view was completely different from how I experienced those same events in my life.

When I recovered from my shock, I told my sister that I felt I had not only learned something essential from each idea I had nurtured, but that in my view what mattered was that they had helped or touched others and were all important building blocks toward greater success and my ability to reach the world in the ways I knew I needed to. She was equally surprised to hear my perspective, but I believe she understood me. I still have no regrets about anything I have tried, or anyone I have aligned with. Even when someone has bitterly disappointed me as a business partner, I have used the experience as an opportunity to become more self-reliant, and to place more value my own worth and abilities. We always have a choice in how we view our circumstances, and those choices have a real effect on our personal happiness and our ability to achieve emotional stability and success.

Further good news is that the benefits of mindfulness and self-compassion go beyond a positive mood. Again I will refer to the work being done at The Greater Good Science Center at UC Berkeley, which offers a course on the Science of Happiness and a set of happiness tools on their website, "Greater Good in Action."[46] Their research concludes that happiness and good health go hand in hand. The associated health benefits are important for each of us individually, and can and should be part of any corporate strategy for increased employee well-being that will result in positive engagement and lower medical expenses for the company.

Resilience and Well-Being

We live stressful lives, and when we are triggered constantly, stress builds up and can overpower us. Under stress, our reactivity dominates our positivity, and we may not feel very resilient. The good news is that we can learn to be more resilient—in fact, resilience is one of four components of well-being that are supported by neuroscience to be trainable. This conclusion comes from Dr. Richard Davidson of the University of Wisconsin's Center for Healthy Minds (yes, the same Richard Davidson who did the research with Matthieu Ricard). In Davidson's own words, "Well-being is fundamentally no different than learning to play the cello."[47] Resilience, along with mental outlook, and attention, can be developed through practice, and engaging in this practice will actually change your brain in positive ways.

Resilience is your ability to get up and brush yourself off after you have been knocked down by life. Some people naturally bounce back from adversity more quickly than others, and Davidson wanted to study whether mindfulness meditation could alter the neural circuits involved in resilience and increase that capacity. The research he conducted at the Center for Healthy Minds shows that mindfulness meditation will indeed increase resilience, but long-term mindfulness practice will have the greatest impact.[48] So meditation practice, for most of us, is only part of the answer to greater resilience. According to another study, having purpose in your life helps you to be able to "reframe stressful situations more positively."[49] This finding reinforces the importance of finding a way to align our daily work with meaningful purpose, and not only shows us that purpose creates more engagement, as discussed in an earlier chapter, but also that it adds to our resilience capacity.

Having optimism, a positive attitude, and being able to learn from your failures are all intimately connected to being kind to yourself when you feel down. These practices take very little time to start having an effect on your outlook. In another study done in 2012 at the Center for Healthy Minds, thirty non-meditators received compassion training over a two-week period. This training resulted in observable changes in their brains and also increased behaviors that benefit others, such as helping, sharing, and cooperating.[50]

This recommendation for how to develop resilience may seem quite familiar, as the process is almost the same as summarized in an earlier Micro-Practice, "Leaning into Happiness." The first step is to exercise your mindfulness and begin to manage your stress or upset by recognizing what you are feeling. You can stop and take few mindful breaths, shift your mood by taking a brief walk outside, or even open up a mindfulness app on your phone, such as Headspace, Whil, or Simple Habit, that provides brief guided meditations.

After you have paused, you will have the ability to cognitively see what you were emotionally feeling, and this ability to engage your thinking brain will allow you to shift your perspective. You can then cultivate self-compassion, which has been proven to shift the brain to a more positive outlook. If you practice kindness to yourself on a regular basis, you will find that you are strengthening your resilience and enjoying a greater sense of balance, even when faced with challenges.

Micro-Practice: Developing Resilience

- Take a mindful pause: take a few breaths, step outside, or do a short meditation practice.
- When you have calmed down, look at the situation with more clarity and understanding.
- Without judgment, send yourself loving kindness and realize you were doing your best at that moment. Be spacious and generous to yourself.
- Use the episode as a stepping stone, and allow yourself to feel good that you learned from the experience.

From the field of positive psychology comes one more story of how positive emotions and loving kindness meditation can affect our long-term resilience, well-being, and happiness. Barbara Fredrickson, psychologist and professor at the University of North Carolina, Chapel Hill, wanted to test her hypothesis that an individual's personal resources, such as increased mindfulness, purpose in life, and resilience, would compound over time if positive emotions could be continuously aroused. She hypothesized, and through her study observed, that Loving Kindness Meditation is a strategy that could produce these results.

The study took place in a workplace setting as a seven-week wellness workshop in which participants practiced Loving Kindness Meditation—the form of compassion meditation we've been exploring in this chapter—daily. Her conclusion was that "by elevating daily experiences of positive emotions, the practice of Loving Kindness Meditation led to long-term gains that made genuine differences in people's lives."[51]

To me, this is hopeful, and also serves as inspiration for practicing and applying mindfulness and compassion meditation in our personal and professional worlds. We can change our brain circuitry, feel more joyful, and make a difference in our own lives and others' lives by practicing loving kindness toward ourselves. We can thrive by transforming our setbacks into resilience and gained experience.

CHAPTER 6:

Connect and Succeed

Important to the success of a leader or a business is the ability to feel and respond to the needs of the larger whole—clients, customers, vendors, team members, and shareholders—and not just to individual desires and ambitions. When I started my career in business, I consulted for a firm that specialized in helping rapidly growing companies make the transition to a more professionally managed organization. As we looked at improving systems to accommodate growth, we discovered that the core challenge facing these changing companies was their people; more specifically, the individuals who were being moved up from positions of personal achievement, where no one was reporting to them, to roles where they would be managing others.

A national aerospace company invited us to coach one of their new managers, Sue, who was having a difficult time in her role. Sue had been excited about her promotion. She was known as the top HR trainer in the company, and had worked there for four years. Her boss was leaving and she been promoted to his

Director of Training position. Six weeks later, she wasn't sure she had made the right decision. Her former friends and colleagues, now her direct reports, were complaining that she was aloof. She, meanwhile, was feeling a bit jealous of them as she reviewed their accomplishments from the perspective of her new role; she missed the "performance" aspect of training, and wasn't so sure she knew how to handle her feelings about her peers and the lack of public attention in her new role. Her colleagues did not know how to handle the change in relationship either, and found it hard to take feedback from her. They resented her management style, which tended to highlight the power she had over them. She scheduled meetings when they were convenient for her, set agendas and ran those meetings without asking for input, and insisted on reviewing her teams' training presentation slides and making "improvements" to them. Sue was still thinking like an individual rather than collaborating. She wasn't helping her team develop trust in her.

Many of the new managers we were working with, like Sue, were "stars" in their field who had been promoted due to excelling at self-sufficiency and singular focus—traits that were not defining aspects of success in their new roles. They had enjoyed receiving praise for producing results that they controlled, and now, in their new roles as managers, many of them assumed that the people who worked for them should simply follow their orders. In general, this attitude would not make anyone very popular, yet many of these individuals were sincerely surprised when they received feedback from their peers that they needed improvement in their relational skills. They had found success thus far by following the track of individual excellence, but they had reached the point where more was needed.

To start with, there were managerial skills to learn. But even before that, there was a need for a new mindset. My colleagues and I needed to help these new managers learn to think about others, to make the shift from thinking about "me" to thinking about "we." This was not a quick process, and it involved training, coaching, and helping the managerial teams develop openness to feedback. As we worked together, they began to think of themselves as a member of a team and not just an individual. In doing so, they found a new kind of success.

We Are a Social Species

The word compassion means "to suffer with," or "to suffer together." Compassion is a feeling of sympathy that is accompanied by an overwhelming desire to do something about what you are feeling. Scientists studying compassion are discovering that this feeling has deep biological roots, suggesting an evolutionary purpose for this emotion. This line of thought actually began with Darwin, who wrote in his book *The Descent of Man* that sympathy was a determining factor for the selection of who would survive. In fact, he hypothesized that natural selection would favor "the most sympathetic members, (who) would flourish best, and rear the greatest number of offspring."[52]

That compassion for each other is one of our strongest instincts may seem counterintuitive considering our combative office environments, let alone the human atrocities we hear about each day. However, at the most basic level, our very existence on the planet has depended upon our ability to care for one another. Human babies, with their big heads and large brains relative to their bodies, cannot survive to adulthood on their own. Dachner Keltner of the Greater Good Science Center, in a video on the evolutionary roots of compassion, said about the human head size, "and that simple fact changed everything. It rearranged our social structures, building cooperative networks of caretaking, and it rearranged our nervous systems. We became the super caregiving species, to the point where acts of care improve our physical health and lengthen our lives. We are born to be good to each other."[53]

Darwin offered an explanation for the origin of compassion, writing, "We are impelled to relieve the sufferings of another, in order that our own painful feelings may be at the same time relieved." He continued, "In however complex a manner this feeling may have originated . . . those communities, which included the greatest number of the most sympathetic members, would flourish best."[54] His remarks imply that when people in social networks have cooperative ties to each other, they do better.

In addition to ensuring survival, kindness and compassion have also been shown to be contagious. A 2015 study published in the journal *Biological Psychology* investigated the warm feeling we get when we witness the kindness of someone alleviating another's pain. The name that researchers have given to this high we experience when we witness human goodness is "moral elevation." During times of "moral elevation," we simultaneously experience the stress response of the sympathetic nervous system (fight and flight) and the calming response of the parasympathetic nervous system (warm feelings and bonding behavior). This dual activation is unusual, and the only other situations in which it's been observed are parenting and sexual activity. S.R. Saturn, one of the researchers on the study, theorizes that the warm feeling we get comes from the hormone oxytocin being released, which gives us a strong visceral response and makes us want to repeat the action to feel it again.[55]

Since so much of the pervasive suffering at work is caused by feelings of being ignored, judged, or not recognized for our contributions, you can be an important source of its relief by offering very simple acts of kindness. You have tremendous power to uplift those with whom you come into contact, moment by moment.

Each of us has the ability to be kind to at least one person every day by offering a smile, genuine praise, or even a simple hello. The effects of your openness will be contagious. Society is composed of myriad personal exchanges that occur each moment, and we can choose to engage in a positive connection rather than pull away.

Mary E., a participant in one of my classes, was profoundly affected by the kindness of a work colleague. She shared this story with me:

> *I reentered the workplace in 2000 after an eight-year period during which I suffered from a debilitating major depression and suicidality. I recovered and went to work for the Massachusetts Rehabilitation Commission, which helps people with disabilities find jobs. Some events at work would trigger me and would end with me in tears, not knowing what to do. One of the secretaries, a very proper Italian woman, took pity on me, and when she saw I was getting upset she'd whisk me out of the office and walk me until I stopped crying and had myself together again. She would also come in my office and talk to me every morning for a few minutes to see how I was. I don't think I could have done it without her. We weren't the type of people who would ever be friends because we were too different—she was just being kind. We had a close but strange relationship. She was always there when I needed her and I got better at handling the stresses at work. I retired after a successful fourteen years of her support.*

Our culture's current focus on the individual, on our own achievement as an overriding goal, seems like an anomaly given what we know about how we evolved. The pervasive me-as-number-one values cannot sustain a culture of thriving in an ever-changing VUCA (volatile, uncertain, complex, and ambiguous) world. To solve today's issues, we need to be able to see and feel the bigger context in which our actions are taking place, and utilize the power of social connection. In stories like Mary's, we see that this connection has never gone away, and when we can acknowledge and celebrate our goodness to each other, we strengthen those bonds.

Shifting from "Me" to "We"

A few years ago the head of Shambhala, the spiritual tradition I follow, wrote and recorded a rap song that was pretty cool. The name of the song is "What About Me," and it traces the obsession we have with finding happiness in personal satisfaction, and how that actually gets it backward. The lyrics begin with these words:

> "What about me? That's my first thought every morning.
> What happened to me is the last thought every night.
> Has this gotten me anywhere, any more friends, any
> more love, more joy?
> It should have by now.
> In fact, by now I should be a bundle of joy, because I
> say this mantra every day.
> What about me?"[56]

The song's conclusion is that thinking only about our own needs is never what brings us, or others, happiness or joy. In a famous quote the Dalai Lama says, "We all have to live together, so we might as well live together happily." He sums up why thinking only about "me" doesn't work, and where the solution lies, in *The Art of Happiness*, where he says, "If you want others to be happy, practice compassion. If you want to be happy, practice compassion."[57] If practicing compassion will help us to live together happily, that sounds like a great method for shifting from "me" to "we." Let's take a look at how we can take an active role in arousing our innate human compassion.

In Chapter 5, we did a version of Loving-Kindness practice for self-compassion. We will now expand this basic meditation to allow our caring nature to include everyone. Try this exercise on your own at home, as regularly as you can, for ten to fifteen minutes at a time and see how its effects permeate your day and week.

Practice: Loving-Kindness Meditation

1. Take a comfortable, relaxed, and alert sitting posture and breathe naturally. If you are comfortable doing so, close your eyes.

2. Place your attention on your heart area and, if it helps to ignite your caring feelings, begin by bringing to mind a person or possibly an animal that you love. Allow this image to stimulate your natural feelings of tenderness and care. Notice the feeling of warmth and allow it to spread out from your heart to fill your body as you send love in this practice.

3. First, send love and care to **yourself** by saying silently:
      May I be well; may I be happy
      May I feel safe, may I be at peace
      May I be free from suffering
      May I feel loved and cared for

(continued on next page)

(continued from previous page)

4. Then, bring to mind **someone that you care about, love, or respect** and send them love:

May you be well; may you be happy
May you feel safe, may you be at peace
May you be free from suffering
May you feel loved and cared for

5. Next, bring to mind **someone you feel neutral about,** such as a clerk who works at a store or someone you have seen on a bus or at a restaurant, and send them loving feelings:

May you be well; may you be happy
May you feel safe, may you be at peace
May you be free from suffering
May you feel loved and cared for

6. Then, bring to mind **someone who irritates you** and send them love. (At a gathering I attended with the Dalai Lama, he mentioned that he always brought along on his travels a monk he found particularly irritating, for just this purpose!)

May you be well; may you be happy
May you feel safe, may you be at peace
May you be free from suffering
May you feel loved and cared for

7. Bring to mind someone you consider **an "enemy," someone who may have hurt you** or acted against you, and send them love if you can by repeating:

May you be well; may you be happy
May you feel safe, may you be at peace
May you be free from suffering
May you feel loved and cared for

8. Include **all the people in the world**, people you don't even know who are suffering with war, hunger, disease, and poverty. Wish them well and send out your love and warmth to cover the globe:

> *May you be well; may you be happy*
> *May you feel safe, may you be at peace*
> *May you be free from suffering*
> *May you feel loved and cared for*

9. Return your attention to feeling your body breathing and allow yourself to enjoy the feelings of love and warmth that have been generated. When you are ready, slowly open your eyes.

Through regular practice, you may find that you have established new, gentler habits that replace your previous reactions. If you become accustomed to *imagining* sending kindness to irritating people and enemies, then at work, when you find yourself with a difficult person or getting angry, you can remember this meditation and "flash" loving kindness to the individual on the spot. (See the practice below for more information on how to do this.) You are actually rewiring your brain and creating new neural pathways when you practice this meditation, to the point where seeing someone you previously disliked can become a trigger for kindness!

Micro-Practice: Flashing Kindness

Feeling irritated with someone, being in an argument, or even dreading an encounter that's about to take place are all good times to "flash" on loving-kindness. Flashing refers to acknowledging the feeling of irritation and using that as a reminder to extend kindness. If you have become accustomed to arousing interest and care through regular Loving-Kindness practice, you may be able to allow feelings of irritation or dislike that arise in any given moment at work to trigger an opening rather than closing of your heart. You can actually grow circuits in your brain that make an association between feeling aggressive toward someone and wishing them well. This may seem awkward at first, but with practice it becomes easier—and it feels much better than feeling threatened or angry.

Empathy And Compassion

Empathy is the ability to experience and understand what another feels while remaining clear about the distinction between your feelings and theirs. We can think of empathy as "putting yourself in the shoes of another," while compassion moves into doing something to alleviate any suffering you feel from empathy.

There are many times when we may feel overwhelmed by another's suffering, and instead of opening we shut down. This happens when we don't allow for a distinction between our own feelings and another's. Without that distinction, feeling what others feel can simply be "emotional contagion," meaning that you're absorbing another person's energy or emotions simply because they're in the field. Your ability to empathize with others without emotional contagion develops as a result of having developed self-awareness about what you feel and why you feel it. The practices of mindful meditation, personal reflection, and body scan, which help you get in touch with your emotions in your body, are all a part of the process of strengthening your ability to empathize. The better you understand your own feelings, the more you can understand those of others. Through practice, you can increase your empathy capacity.

There is a scientifically established connection between a person's self-awareness and the amount of empathy they experience for others. The neuroscientific reason for this is that the empathy component of compassion is "wired" into our brains. A 2006 study by Jean Decety and Claus Lamm showed that similar neurons fire when we process our own emotions and when we understand someone else's emotions.[58] In other words, when we see another person in pain, the neuronal pattern in our brain looks as if we are personally experiencing the emotion. We feel what they are feeling, which is the "putting ourselves in their shoes" component of empathy. But the greater our self-awareness, the more we understand what we are experiencing emotionally, and that it is not our experience but that of another. These findings also explain how we have the power to increase our personal emotional intelligence (EQ), an important factor in leadership success that's directly related to our ability to open our hearts and minds to others and understand them. (We will talk more about this in Chapter 7.)

In a related but accidental finding by scientists at the University of Parma, "mirror neurons" were discovered in monkeys' brains. Scientists in the lab had placed electrodes in the monkeys' brains to record neural activity, like what happens when a monkey reaches to pick up food. One day, a researcher looked up at the monitor as he was eating his sandwich and noticed a monkey looking at him. The monkey was not eating, but the same neural pathways could be seen firing on the monkey's brain scan image as if it were. The scientists repeated this as a controlled experiment and found the same results: witnessing another person making an action activated the neurons in the brain that would have fired had the individual (or monkey, in this case) been the one performing the action.

This study might explain why we feel such strong emotions when watching a movie of someone being harmed, even though we know it is a film, or why we feel upset at work when we witness a colleague being shamed or yelled at: mirror neurons are firing inside our own brains as if the act were happening to us. This also reinforces how self-awareness and being able to distinguish our own feelings from another's can help.

We can't control our environment in the workplace, just as we cannot control the multiple emotional situations we are exposed to day after day. But when we are able to empathize with others, and understand what they are feeling without getting caught up in taking on their feelings personally, we are in a better position to be of comfort and to maintain our own equanimity. When we don't have to shut off our feelings for fear of being overwhelmed, we are also better able to make ourselves available to the good feelings that come to us in the course of a workday, and that leads to happiness and well-being.

Compassion takes us beyond empathy and into a desire to take action on what we feel is happening to another. It has been defined by Thupten Jinpa of Stanford CCARE as "a mental state endowed with a sense of concern for the suffering of others and aspiration to see that suffering relieved."[59] Compassion contains two of the dimensions found in empathy: 1) a feeling of concern for another, and 2) a cognitive component of seeking to understand the other. The desire to relieve another's suffering, which is the human instinct that's allowed our species to survive, is an additional factor that separates compassion from empathy.

This desire to be helpful, and wishing for the relief of suffering, are very powerful agents of our personal happiness. It was in fact this very practice of compassion that resulted in Matthieu Ricard's exceptionally positive brain scan. Chad Meng Tan is the author of *Search Inside Yourself* which chronicles the application of mindfulness and emotional intelligence programs at Google. In the book, Meng quotes Ricard describing the feeling of happiness that results from compassion practice as "a deep sense of flourishing that arises from an exceptionally healthy mind . . . not a mere pleasurable feeling, a fleeting emotion, or a mood, but an optimal state of being."[60]

If we are looking for the ability to understand and respond to others while staying grounded in well-being and emotional stability, the practice of compassion can help us reconnect with our optimal state of being, the happiness of a healthy mind.

Overcoming "Us" and "Them"

Part of the compassion instinct that has allowed us to survive as a species also has the effect of causing us to bond more naturally and easily with people we consider to be part of our "tribe"—our group or community—which might be ethnic, social, or political. Andrea Serino, now a senior scientist at University Hospital, Lausanne, undertook a study in 2009 with a team of other scientists when she was at the University of Parma, Italy, called "I Feel What You Feel if You Are Similar to Me," demonstrating that our empathy is affected by whether we feel that someone else is in our "in-group" or not.[61]

In order to examine how we respond to people who are either similar to or different from us, researchers in this study used a phenomena called "visual remapping of touch" to explore their theory of similarity. "Visual remapping of touch" is a process whereby a person is shown an image of themselves being touched while at the same time being physically touched in that same spot. It's been proven that simulating touch through an image of ourselves makes us feel the touch more strongly. So if you are looking at a video of your face being stroked while your cheek is simultaneously being stimulated, you will actually feel that stimulation more strongly because the viewing of the image makes the sensation more acute.

In Serino's study, they wanted to test if this effect worked if a subject was looking at a face that was not their own. The purpose of the experiment was to test social connection and empathy. They used a stimulation on the cheek that was so faint as to be undetectable as they showed test subjects the images they'd chosen.

What they discovered was that if the study subject was looking at a face that was from their same ethnic group, they reported feeling the stroke on their cheek, the same as they did if they were watching a video of their own face. But if the face on the video being stroked was that of a person of different ethnic group, the subject did not report detecting the electronic stimulation at all or as definitely. This showed that at an unconscious neurological level, our physical empathy system and our response to others is affected by whether or not we identify with that person as part of our "in-group." To me, the important takeaway of this study has to do with the necessity of widening our circle of empathy. If we work to develop the mental habits of seeing more people as similar to ourselves, we can aim to expand our "in-group" to include more people.

Unfortunately, it's all too easy in the world and workplace to solely identify with people who look like us and think like us, and to ignore or dismiss the others. When we do this, however, we may not be able to feel empathy for those we consider different, and this no longer works in our multicultural reality. Loving-Kindness Meditation is one way in which we can create new mental habits of kindness and acceptance. In the following practice, "Just Like Me," we actively remember that every single person has the same desire to be happy and free from suffering as we do. It helps to actually contemplate this fact, and to say the lines of the practice in order to connect with people we may consider to be "other." In doing so, we can train ourselves to widen our sense of who constitutes "us."

Practice: Just Like Me

Begin this meditation by taking a comfortable, relaxed, and alert posture and becoming present to your body and your breathing. Let yourself relax, and then bring to mind someone you consider to be different than you. You might think of someone who comes from another part of the world, from a different religion, or a different belief system. This may be someone from a different ethnic group who dresses and looks completely different from you, or from a different political party. Once you have them in mind, begin the following contemplation, pausing to consider what you are saying as you view the individual in question:

This person is a human being with a body and a mind, just like me.
This person has feelings, emotions, and thoughts, just like me.
This person has a family, friends, and relatives in their life, just like me.
This person has, at some point in his or her life, been sad, disappointed, angry, hurt, or confused, just like me.

(continued on next page)

(continued from previous page)

> This person has, in his or her life, experienced physical and
> emotional pain and suffering, just like me.
> This person wishes to be free from pain and suffering, just
> like me.
> This person wishes to be healthy and loved, and to have
> fulfilling relationships, just like me.
> This person wishes to be happy, just like me.

Empathy may be a part of our mental "wiring," but exercising it is also a choice we make. We can choose to extend ourselves to others beyond our limited comfort zone.

In a March 2013 *New York Times* "Corner Office" interview, Adam Bryant spoke with the director of the NeuroLeadership Institute, David Rock, and Rock presented another perspective on the part our brains play in segregating everyone at work into "us" and "them." He said, "The brain divides everything into two categories: rewards and threats. That's why it's crucial for managers to make their employees feel that they're on the same team."[62] Rock believes that unless a leader makes an effort to ensure that team members feel included, the simple occurrence of a boss walking into the room can activate everyone else's sense of threat. His theory is that employees can feel a sense of lowered status and greater uncertainty because they contrast themselves to their bosses.

Rock made suggestions in this article about how people in positions of leadership can address this situation. He uses the acronym SCARF to describe five issues he has identified as affecting people's behavior at work, and which may create feeling "in" or "out." In SCARF, S stands for status, discussed as a feeling of potential threat from the boss just walking into the room. C stands for certainty. To address certainty, Rock recommends adopting an open-book-management approach, making all financials available to everyone in order to reduce uncertainty. A is for autonomy, or a sense of control. A leader needs to recognize that employees can feel threatened unless the leader makes it clear to them that their opinion matters and will affect the outcome of decisions. R is for relatedness. If employees feel respected, and feel like they share goals with their superiors, then everyone can feel like they are in the "in-group." The importance of feeling that you are in the same "in-group" is that if you feel that you are on the same team as your boss, you process what he or she is saying with the same networks as you do when thinking your own thoughts. This is the effect that was demonstrated in the Serino study above—a feeling of relatedness that is actually the neurology of trust, teamwork, and collaboration. The importance of seeing your colleagues as similar to you, and of helping your team and teammates to feel accepted, is crucially important to success and happiness at work.

Compassion in Business

About twenty years ago, I was faced with a conflict. My father was retiring and being honored by Duke University in North Carolina on the very same weekend that I needed to be at another life-honoring ceremony for a close friend in Oregon. I was actually invited to speak at both events, so it was a big conflict. After much agonizing, I finally figured out a way to do both by attending my dad's party on Friday night and leaving before sunrise on Saturday morning from Raleigh to fly to Oregon. It was a complex routing that would take me to Texas and San Francisco before finally landing me in Ashland, and the timing was tight.

When I got to Texas they announced a delay, and then the delay got longer, and I could see that I would miss the last leg of my trip if I didn't get on a different flight. Practically in tears from exhaustion and stress, I went to the desk and explained my situation to the woman working there. She smiled and said she would be right back. About ten minutes later she came back and said, "Follow me, please." She led me through the airport to the desk of a competing airline, produced cash out of her pocket, and bought me a ticket on the next direct flight to San Francisco! She personally arranged for the transfer of my luggage, wished me a good flight, and was off. I was blown away by her kindness, and have been a loyal and happy customer of Southwest Airlines ever since.

Compassionate management practices can certainly create devoted customers, but they also have significant benefits inside of a company. We see simple compassionate actions at work regularly, such as people staying late to help a colleague finish a task, giving help to a new employee, or covering someone's shift on short notice. When managers and leaders guide from compassionate values, they generate greater loyalty, commitment, and trust in their employees, which then leads to better performance, individually and for the company.

Organizational Compassion

To make a profound change in organizational culture, the practices of compassion must grow beyond the actions of individuals to become a part of the way in which the organization operates. In a 2004 article titled "Compassion in Organizational Life," researchers from the University of Michigan and the University of British Columbia looked at how empathy and compassion operate in collective systems. The article posited that organizations have the capacity to develop systems or protocols for the collective noticing of pain, feeling of emotion, and compassionate responding.[63]

This article offers Cisco Systems as an example of an organization with policies that create this collective capacity for compassion. CEO John Chamber has a policy that he is to be notified, within forty-eight hours, of every instance in which a Cisco employee or an employee's immediate family member falls seriously ill or passes away. This policy encourages employees to be on the lookout for pain, especially a colleague's grief. The policy also expresses the organizational value that people's family circumstances are worthy of concern, making it more likely that members will share painful family news. The policy also clearly defines what type of pain to look out for (in this case, grief). Cisco has a communication system in place called the Serious Health Notification System that enables such information to reach the CEO quickly. As you can see, this policy integrates many systems and policies that allow organizational noticing to take place.

Collective feeling can take place in an organization that allows emotions and stories about home and work life to be freely shared. An example of how this can become an organizational practice is when team meetings are places where members are allowed and encouraged to share what is going on with them in their lives, as well as with their work tasks. This kind of open communication and sharing creates an environment in which pain is tolerated and colleagues' support can be appreciated.

Organizations vary in their capacity for collective responding, and leadership and corporate cultural values play a key role in those responses. A wonderful example of a compassionate response to a crisis of pain in the workplace comes from Bill Ford, former CEO of Ford Motors. In a 2013 interview from

Wisdom 2.0 with Jack Kornfield, Bill Ford shared how each day he set his intention to face whatever arose with compassion and loving kindness. At one point, just as he had taken over as CEO, there was a major explosion at the Ford River Rouge plant. Ford headed over immediately, and personally spent months going to hospital rooms, homes, and funerals. He asked himself what else he could do, and decided to give credit cards to all families affected so that they could cover their needs. He said that his lawyers had a fit when he did that, because they thought it would expose the company to future lawsuits. Instead, it engendered great good will and letters of gratitude, and, as Ford shared, "There are bonds with the families I still keep now."[64]

Cultivating Empathy and Compassion for Customers

Tier1 Performance Solutions is an unusual creative consultancy that works to improve organizations through the performance of their people. It does this in many ways, including by creating beautiful visual games, videos, and stories that engage employees in innovative ways to learn what their company wishes to communicate. I was privy to two of Tier1's recent client projects, and both are stunning examples of corporate materials that educate and communicate a culture of empathy, compassion, and appreciation.

The first project is an interactive game designed for employees of AbbVie, a global pharmaceutical company committed to patient-centered innovation. The employees of AbbVie play this game to develop empathy and understanding for the patients they serve. As a player, the employee is the patient, navigating the journey of having psoriasis. A psoriasis patient suffers on several levels—physically, emotionally, and socially—as a result of their constant rashes. The clever video game allows for multiple choices on each of these different physical, emotional, and social paths, all of which lead the player to experience the life events of the patient. The game was designed because, AbbVie says, "Empathy is at the core of serving our customers."

The second project is called the Humana Plum Book, made for Humana Inc., a Kentucky-based health insurance company that serves over 13 million customers in the US. The Plum Book is a beautiful video aimed at inspiring the Humana employees to share their stories of living out Humana's values, and going the extra distance to serve their customers. Humana hopes that by spreading and sharing these inspiring stories, their employees will meet the company goal of "making every community they serve 20 percent healthier by 2020."

Success with Compassion

Room 214, a twelve-year-old digital marketing and social media agency with thirty-eight employees, is a success story. It's a vibrant company whose values span the spectrum of the seven levels of organizational consciousness discussed in Chapter 5. They exhibit financial stability, harmonious relationships, high performance, continuous renewal and learning, shared values and vision, and strategic alliances and partnerships, and they seek to be of service to their clients while operating with compassion. They are happy at work! But it wasn't always this way.

Three years ago, Room 214's CEO, James Clark, had lost the spark. After a summer break with his family, he realized he wasn't looking forward to going back to work. He was shocked, since this was his company. He'd started it, and had always had so much passion for it; how could he be feeling this way? He told his business partner, Jason, that he just wasn't feeling like coming into work. "It's a slog," he admitted. Jason said he was having the same experience, so they agreed something had to be done.

His first day back, James decided to visit one of their customers and pick up some materials directly from their client's workplace, which was located about forty minutes away. When he walked into his customer's office, he was stunned. He described the energy as being "like a ray of sunshine coming down." He had to know what was going on. The owner shared his company's commitment to an open-book management system where every employee could see and understand all the business issues, decisions, and results. He explained how all of his employees were engaged in "owning" the results and running the business. He told James that he'd learned this system from a training program that had originated at Zingerman's Deli in Ann Arbor, Michigan. For years, Zingerman's has been widely praised for its products and world-class customer service, and they now share their secrets to success through a training they offer to other companies.[65]

James and Jason took the ZingTrain program and fully embraced its philosophy of "massive transparency" and "being compassionate to people." They redesigned their approach to their business in 2013, at which point they also created a 2020 vision.

Room 214's new mantra is, "Creating Valuable Relationships." Their three core values are: Doing our Best, Acting Out of Love Instead of Fear, and Leading with Humility. These powerful intentions have led to considerable success, and the business is well on its way to achieving all of their 2020 goals.

They were told it would take three to four years to get good at open-book management (OBM), and that's been true. As they entered into their fourth year, however, they told me they're seeing the financial benefits of that transparent and participatory system. They have seen a steady increase in top-line revenue since they implemented the system, from 5 percent to 23 percent in just three years.

But James and Jason are interested in tracking more than financials. They have put into place employee training and mentoring programs, and they track those performance metrics as well. They have a Giving Back line where they track employees' individual volunteer hours, as well as pounds of food and money donated to charitable events.

They also have a line on their board for tracking company progress called Client Love, where they track the amount of times a client has mentioned that they "love" Room 214's work, ideas, or simply working with them. (The board is also the place where all of the open-book information is available to all company members.) James and Jason say they see a direct correlation between the amount of client love they receive and profit increases.

In James's words, "It's those non-financial lines where our internal focus is, because we know those are the sprockets that drive the gears, that move the company." Employee retention at Room 214 is 85 percent, where the industry average is 70 percent. About this James says, "What's important is we celebrate those 15 percent who choose to move, as most of them are pursuing opportunities they could have only dreamed about prior to working at Room 214."

Whether you are a large corporation trying to improve our national wellness or a small company improving the lives of its employees and their customers, engaging with empathy and compassion leads to greater success, fulfillment, health, and joy for employees and customers alike.

CHAPTER 7:

Radiate Confidence

The stories and practices in the previous chapters demonstrate the power of becoming self-aware, of being willing to investigate and face your own fears, and of moving from the pain of self-criticism or self-absorption to loving self-acceptance and compassion for others. With greater curiosity about what is possible, and having taken some steps down the path from head to heart, you are integrating your intellect and intuition and uncovering your inner, vast self—your true nature.

Although the word "vast" may seem dramatic, it's actually simply pointing to the extent of opportunity that is yours to tap. This foundation of being, this goodness of your essence, is always there, and now you are aware of the possibilities. By setting your intention to reconnect with your nature and having the courage to practice shifting your habits, you can now glimpse, or at least envision, the aspect of yourself that radiates power and confidence, and that will allow your intentions for positive change to manifest. This is the place of your innate confidence, the most authentic expression of you, unblocked by limiting habits, reactions, and beliefs. When you radiate this confidence, there is little you cannot accomplish.

I remember a time when I had the privilege to be traveling with a magnetic person who was also deeply self-aware. He was the protégé of the CEO of a major transformational seminar organization I represented, and we were on our way from Los Angeles to New York City for a big meeting, traveling first class on a red-eye flight. I was young at the time, so it did not seem so difficult to stay up all night drinking the free cocktails and enjoying the novelty of a first-class trip across the country. It was a long flight, and we were the only ones awake, and the stewardess was almost overly attentive to us. Finally, she burst out with the question that must have been on her mind since the start of the flight. She looked directly at my companion and said, "Who are you? I know you are someone very special and important, I just can't place it!" What she was responding to was the aura of genuine confidence, ease, and joy that he naturally radiated. My companion laughed gently and said, "I am no one special, just enjoying the flight. I'm feeling good, so you might be catching that!"

Unconditional Confidence

There's a common expression: We know it when we see it. But in actuality, we know it when we *feel* it. The person in front of you is radiating energy, excitement, and enthusiasm, and at the same time is calm, grounded, and self-possessed. The confident individual is magnetic to us. We want to get to know her, and may be curious about what she does and how she became that way.

Unconditional confidence is distinguishable from feigned confidence or arrogance. Its nature is gentle and spontaneous.

This kind of confidence is the simple result of being genuinely comfortable within your own skin. You know your strengths and weaknesses, and not only accept but lovingly offer yourself to the world just as you are, with nothing to hide. With this kind of self-knowledge comes clarity—around what you have to offer the world and what opportunities to pursue and knowledge to seek.

This kind of clarity leads to confidence in decision-making. Knowing what to accept and what to reject are no longer huge dilemmas because you are able to trust what you know and what you sense emotionally—an ability we all possess. Something within is always guiding us to the truest choice. When you are at peace with yourself, you can feel or hear that message, and not resist. The radiance that exudes from the genuinely confident individual is your own brilliant mind, unobstructed by self-doubt and needless inner debates about what to do and which way to turn.

The following practice is a way to evoke a connection to this space in our being that we may have forgotten how to access. This is a guided meditation. You can have someone read it to you, you can record it for yourself, or you can listen to it on my website.[66]

Practice: Unconditional Confidence

- Get comfortable and take a few deep breaths.
- Close your eyes, and move your awareness from your head—from your thinking mind—to your heart.
- Rest and breathe, feeling the heart of your being. Your heart is tender, warm, and open.
- Feel curious about yourself and the world outside of you.
- The warmth from your heart radiates as love in all directions and the world you experience mirrors back that love.

(continued on next page)

(continued from previous page)

- Now imagine that your heart transforms into the sun. You are brilliant, radiant, magnificent, and cannot be contained.
- Your brilliance dispels any shadows, doubt, or depression.
- You feel young, and your joy is unbounded. Everything touches you deeply and genuinely.
- Red is so red, and flowers burst with scent.
- The blue sky is so blue, and it is filled with clouds, animals, chariots, mountain peaks and birds. Anything you can imagine will appear—in fact, anything and everything is possible!
- You live in a magical world!

Do you remember experiencing the world this way? Is there something familiar in this feeling? Does this practice awaken a distant memory, or did you touch this place just recently and wonder how to live like this more regularly?

For each of us, our current connection to our natural state will be different, so our answers to these questions will vary. The contemplation above is meant to evoke unconditional confidence. Feel it. It is your birthright, just waiting to be rediscovered. For some of us, this is great news, and perhaps you can't wait to spend time deepening into this recollection.

For others this meditation might tap into feelings of inadequacy, fear, doubt, and hesitation that have become very familiar, so comfortable and believable that we think that is who we are. When we contemplate our true nature, the brilliance, warmth, and clarity might seem overwhelming. Even though it does seem to be what we have been searching for, we aren't quite sure if we want to go there.

If you're struggling at all, I invite you to drop your hesitation for a little while and see what happens. If you are willing to step out of the familiar, and journey back to the heart of your being, you will reawaken as if from sleep. Your cynicism, doubt, and fear will give way to the delighted wonder of childhood, the warmth of unconditional love, and the genuine confidence of being true to yourself. Radiant confidence is who you are, just waiting to be reclaimed. There is really nothing to do but burn away the clouds we have wrapped ourselves in, and we have the "sun" inside to help us to do it!

Unconditional or radiant confidence is the mark of a successful leader. When you can be both passionate and inspiring, grounded and self-possessed at the same time, you are also wise. Henry David Thoreau said, "It is characteristic of wisdom not to do desperate things." Wisdom comes from within the heart, but also includes a wise outlook, plan, or course of action. Within the wise and confident individual who integrates both their intellect and their intuition, a balance has been achieved. This balance is expressed through our emotional intelligence, which is something we can develop. In fact, you have already begun the process.

Emotional Intelligence

Your Emotional Intelligence (EQ) is your ability to identify and manage your own personal moods and emotions, and also your competence in handling interpersonal relationships. Your EQ is your ability to remain open and aware to the present and whatever is happening, without reactivity. This of course is important while dealing with challenging or unexpected situations, conversations, or individuals. If you can maintain your composure, or your "cool," you can appraise the situation more objectively and come to a proper response. EQ results from intelligently understanding and managing the emotions of yourself and others. It is not a fixed measurement like IQ, but rather a set of skills or competencies you can train. Actually, this kind of training is exactly what this book has been presenting all along.

People with low EQs tend to be reactive, particularly under stress. Their behavior may be become volatile, aggressive, or arrogant. They seem unable to manage themselves, and remain unaware of their effect on others. These kinds of emotional reactive patterns are rooted in our more ancient limbic system, where the amygdala resides. As noted earlier in this book, feelings of emotional reaction occur before our rational brain, or prefrontal cortex, receives the message and has a chance to moderate. When we practice mindfulness, we are creating connections, literally growing billions of new cells, which in turn create networks of neurons that speed up and streamline the communication between the emotional and rational parts of our brain. That increasing ability to engage our rational brain is the basis for expanding our emotional intelligence.

The four skills of EQ are self-awareness, self-management, social awareness, and relationship management. We will look deeply into each of these areas, but first let's explore why EQ is so important for a more successful workplace and a happier personal career.

It should not be surprising that the ability to respond well to constant change, stress, and difficult people and situations has been found to be more important than IQ, personality, or experience in predicting success at work. There are countless studies to support this; when I performed an online search for supporting articles, my query returned 378,000 responses! Now, after decades of research into EQ, it appears that this ability to work intelligently with our emotions is the intangible quality that sets "star" performers apart from the crowd. Travis Bradbury, author of *Emotional Intelligence 2.0*, wrote in a Forbes post:[67]

> *Of all the people we've studied at work, we've found that 90% of top performers are also high in emotional intelligence. On the flip side, just 20% of bottom performers are high in emotional intelligence. You can be a top performer without emotional intelligence, but the chances are slim. . . . The link between emotional intelligence and earnings is so direct that every point increase in emotional intelligence adds $1,300 to an annual salary. These findings hold true for people in all industries, at all levels, in every region of the world. We haven't yet been able to find a job in which performance and pay aren't tied closely to emotional intelligence.*

People with high EQ are better able to adjust to changes, and also better able to work in teams. The number of degrees you hold is less important to your success than whether you are aware, empathetic, respected by others, and able to manage your reactions. In our VUCA (volatile, uncertain, complex, ambiguous) world, EQ may become even more important still as the pace of new technologies and innovations increases exponentially.

Self-Awareness

Self-awareness refers to knowing what you are feeling at any time, and also having an understanding of how you typically react to situations and other people. This kind of awareness may not always be comfortable, because the feelings we have are not all positive. When self-aware, you understand yourself well, and you know your strengths and weaknesses. This is a foundational skill for all of emotional intelligence, and the good news is that the practice of mindfulness—simply noticing your thoughts and emotions as they arise and subside—is the perfect training ground both for developing self-awareness and for strengthening your EQ.

Meditation is one powerful way to strengthen self-awareness, but it's not the only way. Self-awareness is also strengthened by knowing your strengths and weaknesses. Consider going back to two exercises from Chapter 1, "What You Love" and "What I Can Let Go." Feedback from trusted colleagues, a coach, or a mentor can also be a part of your plan to improve your awareness. Nothing teaches us about ourselves more directly than our mistakes. A commitment to learning from failures is a mark of a self-aware individual. Below is a quick check-in with your emotions that you can apply any time while at work, which is yet another way to increase self-awareness.

Micro-Practice: Emotional Check-in

Set an alarm or put a time in your calendar to stop and ask yourself, *What am I feeling right now? Where am I feeling these feelings in my body?* See if you can label your emotion. Is it anger, fear, excitement? Do you know what triggered this feeling? See if you get any information from the emotion. You might want to write down what you noticed.

Self-Management

Self-management results from self-awareness, and refers to the ability to maintain emotional balance when you are feeling strong emotions. Liz, an employee at a consumer products manufacturing company, shared this powerful story with me about her boss, William, who was a top executive at the organization:

Liz and her boss had been working long hours preparing for a presentation at an all-company meeting. The day finally arrived, and William walked onstage to join the CEO and CFO. As he was being introduced by the CFO, the CFO turned to William and said, "Oh, by the way, your project budget has been cut by $1 million dollars." Liz couldn't believe it, and she was further shocked by William's reaction. He didn't say a word. He simply left the stage, and did not return to the meeting. He didn't send any angry e-mails or initiate any conversation about the exchange until they had returned from the conference to their home office. At that time he told Liz, "I just had to leave the situation, and not say anything until I had cooled down. I knew that if I said anything immediately, it could have been terribly damaging, not only to me but to the entire company." Once he was in control and clear about what he wanted to communicate, he addressed the situation. This is an example of really good emotional management.

Social Awareness

Social awareness is connected with empathy, and has to do with being able to pick up on others' unspoken emotions and understand what is going on with them. It requires that we listen well and pay attention to what others are thinking and feeling, which is a skill we need to cultivate. When we use the micro-practice of Active Listening that was offered in Chapter 4, or apply curiosity and mindfulness in meetings, we notice that it takes some effort to place attention on the other person rather than follow the monologue in our own head. When we make that effort, we are developing social awareness.

An empathetic leader understands the individual he or she is addressing, and is able to clearly and appropriately work with people of diverse backgrounds. Because of good listening skills, openness, and genuine curiosity, a person with social awareness can understand the perspectives of those who hold different opinions, and can inspire meaningful dialogue between people of all types.

Relationship Management

The final piece of the EQ puzzle, relationship management, actually brings together all of the previous three EQ competencies. The following story illustrates how Julie, who manages a small product team at a tech company, uses her self-awareness, self-management, and social awareness to successfully manage interactions with her team:

Jim, a member of Julie's staff, had been struggling. He was well liked by his team, but lately had not been performing well, and that was causing friction with his colleagues. Jim regularly missed deadlines and sometimes forgot to follow through with clients. Julie was feeling torn because she knew that Jim's work was frustrating the rest of the team, yet she felt anxious about having a direct conversation with him.

As a first step, Julie realized that she needed to exercise self-awareness and understand what it was about having the conversation that was making her anxious. Using mindfulness, she created the space needed to see her thoughts and feel the physical sensations associated with her emotions. She practiced a few minutes of mindful breathing, followed by compassion practice that allowed her to extend interest and genuine curiosity about why Jim had been struggling and how she might help him. Once grounded in feeling a motivation to help Jim, she felt ready to gently but clearly ask questions to reveal what had been in the way of Jim doing his best work.

She invited Jim to her office and initiated the conversation. "Jim, I am wondering if there is anything that I can help you with. I imagine that there must be something going on in your life that is taking a lot of your attention. I was reluctant to bring this up because I didn't want to add to whatever is bothering you, but your work is suffering, and it's affecting the whole team. I'd like to help you find a solution."

Jim sighed and then said, "I'm really sorry, I didn't realize how bad it had gotten. You're right, my mind is not here at work. I am dealing with a family crisis long-distance. I'm trying to make arrangements for my parents, who live in another state, to move to assisted living. My mother fell and broke her hip, and my dad can't handle what needs to be done. I am constantly getting interrupted by having to deal with all the details. I really should be there with them."

Julie asked him if he would be willing to share this information with the team. He agreed, and once the team understood they created a plan to temporarily split up Jim's responsibilities so that he could take a week to go help his parents make this transition. The team felt good that they could help Jim, and Jim was moved by the compassion of his colleagues.

The skills of relationship management will allow you to diffuse situations of conflict and stress like this at work, which cause so much pain for those who may not yet have the emotional ability to address the problem. As in this example, you can increase and master EQ through practice; even better, once you have developed these competencies, you will likely experience them as natural capacities of your humanity that were within you all along. They are available because they are part of your human goodness, your natural confidence. When your heart is open to yourself and others, you can easily engage in this powerful way with others. (Other important aspects of EQ, and of your open heart, include inspiring, motivating, coaching, and mentoring, which we will be exploring in Chapter 8.)

Invite Creativity, Collaboration, and Innovation

Collaboration, creativity, and innovation are all much more likely to arise when you are confident, relaxed, open, and curious. You have the power to manifest in these ways, and also to be part of establishing a self-aware corporate culture by cultivating these conditions. In this kind of aware culture, problems are acknowledged and not hidden.

Pixar Animation Studios

Ed Catmull, President of Pixar Animation Studios, wrote a book called *Creativity Inc.*, in which he described the company's great success stories of creativity, collaboration, and innovation. "What makes Pixar special," he wrote, "is that we acknowledge we will always have problems, many of them hidden from our view; that we work hard to uncover these problems, even if doing so means making ourselves uncomfortable, and that, when we come across a problem, we marshal all of our energies to solve it."[68]

Pixar was not always the successful movie studio that produced the phenomenally successful movies *Toy Story*, *Finding Nemo*, and *Inside Out*, along with a number of other great animated films. It grew from humbler beginnings, first as a hardware and then a software design company before eventually becoming the successful movie studio it is today. Its growth and success has a lot to do with how its people have faced and learned from problems along the way.

Ed Catmull challenged himself to figure out the particular problem of how to build a sustainable creative culture in his company, because he saw that many other companies failed following their initial successes. He believes that it is leadership's role to identify where they, the leaders, are creating problems and stifling the creative process for their talented staff. Creating the right environment for the flow of creativity is critical, and in his words the best manager "must trust the people they work with and strive to clear the path for them; and always they must pay attention to and engage with anything that creates fear."[69] In his book, he describes the commitment Pixar demonstrates to fearlessly look at problems as opportunities that expose potential for improvement and success. Catmull also indicates the high esteem that Pixar has for its employees, which creates an environment conducive to their success.

Ed Catmull figured out how to build a sustainable creative culture by valuing honesty, excellence, communication, originality and self-assessment. He credits his employees for this possibility. "We were blessed with a remarkable group of employees who valued change, risk, and the unknown and who wanted to rethink how we create," he writes.[70]

In fact, an amazing truth about the creative, collaborative, and innovative success of Pixar Studios is that they use the very forces at play in our VUCA world—change, risk, and the unknown—as ingredients for succeeding. Pixar took an honest look at their strengths and challenges and created a culture of trusting and valuing their people and accepting the risks inherent in creativity. Their approach can be a lesson for any company wishing to encourage innovation and new thinking. Since life and situations are always changing, and since most decisions involve risk and the unknown, encouraging curiosity and creative problem-solving makes those realities an opportunity for growth rather than shutting down in fear and denial. Creating the right environment for their employees to thrive has been key to Pixar's success. In Catmull's words, "A hallmark of a healthy creative culture is that its people feel free to share ideas, opinions, and criticism. Lack of candor, if unchecked, ultimately leads to dysfunctional environments."[71]

Even if your corporate culture is not this awakened, you can use the example of Pixar to find your own creative solutions. As an individual with confidence, you can face and get through any challenge. By inviting the truth, you will have the facts you need to properly assess a situation. If rather than closing yourself off you extend trust to others, you will find that collaboration with colleagues, sometimes outside of your expertise silo, provides a fresh insight and a way to discover new resources and solutions.

The Art of Asking Questions

Recently I was at a leadership conference where we spent a session in special interest groups examining topics of personal interest. The topics were determined by inviting members of the assembly to come forward and post a subject they wished to explore. The rest of the assembly could then choose to join one of the special interest groups. Our assignment was to return to the hall after our small sessions with a powerful question that had arisen out of our discussion. This was quite novel—having the goal of an interaction be to create a question rather than an answer.

When the big group came back together, we all shared our questions, and the effect was powerful. Instead of feeling that we needed to accept or reject anything, an open, collaborative, and spacious discussion session was ignited. Warren Berger, author of *A More Beautiful Question,* wrote in a July 2016 *New York Times* article, "The Power of Why and What If," "Encouraging employees to ask questions can help spur the innovation companies crave." He interviewed Steve Quatrano, a member of the Right Question Institute, who pointed out that formulating questions is a great skill to hone in our changing and dynamic times. Quatrano says that the art of asking questions helps us "to organize our thinking around what we don't know."[72]

Berger suggests training employees to ask more questions by substituting question formulation exercises for more conventional brainstorming sessions. It occurred to me that whoever had designed the exercise in my recent leadership meeting might have read *A More Beautiful Question.* The result for me was one of the most powerful leadership conferences I'd ever attended. In other words, it worked!

Communication Beyond Hope and Fear

When we are being authentic and our communication emanates from unconditional confidence, care, and curiosity, it is possible to establish a ground of trust for exchange with others. This is an outcome both of developing our EQ and tapping into our goodness, our genuine nature. It is particularly important for us to establish this ground of trust when engaged in holding difficult conversations, which have the possibility of bringing up stress and potentially reactive behaviors.

The first step in authentic communication is to become aware of your own motivation in the conversation. Do an "Emotional Check-in," as described earlier in this chapter. What are you feeling? Are you nervous, anxious, angry, needy? Where are you feeling your feelings—in your neck, your shoulders, your belly? Take a few deep breaths and allow yourself to connect with these feelings, and then let your body relax. What information did you get about the importance of this conversation through doing this exercise? Do you understand your emotional response?

You might be able to establish a ground of trust by sharing what you have learned from the self-assessment. For instance, if you realize that you are still feeling angry or upset with a colleague but know you need to put that behind you before you begin working with her on a new project, you might start an exchange by acknowledging your feelings. That conversation might go something like this: "Sarah, I have been feeling awkward about us being put together on this account. I know we had a big disagreement last week about the Conner project, and I guess I have not let it go completely and I'd like to put it behind us. Now that I am aware of how I have been holding on to our fight, I wonder, are you feeling the same way?" This kind of exchange is honest and vulnerable, and shows a willingness to expose yourself and an interest in your colleague's feelings. Your gentleness can open up a fresh space for communication.

The ground of trust begins with trusting yourself. When you let go of your doubts and hesitations by contacting your goodness, you also connect with your compassionate human nature. Having self-respect and a regard for your own worth is a result of the training in gentleness and mindfulness that you have been engaging with throughout the journey of this book. When you are not embarrassed about what you have to say, you can tell the truth, without any deception. Communication of this sort is beyond gentle. It has a power behind it that not only establishes trust but also invites exchange.

Bigger View

When you step into your unconditional confidence, you are letting go of a self-centered perspective and inviting in outrageous possibility. If your intention or motivation for communication with your situation or an individual is not based purely on personal concern, you might be able to let go of hope and fear. You might be surprised to hear me suggesting that you let go of hope; in the sense I am using this word, however, it is simply the flip side of fear—the hoping for something that you fear you will not get. From that perspective, hope and fear are bound up with the narrow view of self-interest, and when that self-interest expresses itself in conversation, it does not engender trust. When you have a bigger view, you can connect with vastness, fearlessness, and your 5,000-foot perspective.

There are several kinds of hope we can learn to recognize, as we will discuss in the following section. When we train ourselves to become familiar with these patterns, we can learn to let them go, and our communication will be freed of these fetters of self-interest. When self-interest is not the motivation for exchange, love and compassion naturally surface and communication, collaboration, and solutions arise.

The Hope Trap

Unfortunately, both hope and fear surface all too often when we are not living in confidence and our most authentic self. And when they're at the root of our communication, they usually discourage genuine communication. They are ways of being that we may not even see because they're so ingrained in us. They are actually just habits, however, and can be released.

There are three common traps of hope that I see most often in my work. The first is poverty mentality. This refers to a feeling of not having enough, which results in hoping to get something for yourself in every exchange. You may experience what does result from your communications as unsatisfying, not enough, since you'd set a higher expectation for the outcome. You may fear that you will not be satisfied, and feel anxious as a result.

The next trap is an attitude of general resentment or aggression as a result of feeling that the world is not the way you hoped it would be. You might enter your communications with this generalized chip on your shoulder, and your attitude of discontent is likely to color your exchanges. Your fear that the world will never give you what you want affects the way you regard the people you are in communication with.

The final trap is hoping to secure your position in a communication because you're invested in proving yourself right. You want to be the winner, come out on top. A hope for this version of achievement leaves little room for genuine exchange. Your fear of not achieving your goal closes you down and leaves no space for you to find out the other person's views, needs, and ideas.

Relaxing into Confidence

All of the traps mentioned above are recipes for anxiety. These self-serving attitudes are at the root of our discontent and our inability to have meaningful exchanges or to create the work environments in which we will thrive. Hopefully with this new understanding we can see that these traps, these attempts to secure a situation with self-interest, are habits that can be recognized and released. These attitudes are a thin covering over our true nature, like clouds over the sun. Our confident nature is vaster than our narrow hopes and fears.

With confidence and trust in yourself, you soar beyond petty perspectives and are naturally open, inquisitive, collaborative, and influential. Your open mind magnetizes and builds bonds with others that enable the formation and execution of shared goals and visions. Communication beyond hope and fear is free of anxiety because you are receptive to change and to the unknown, and are able to thrive in a VUCA world. By radiating confidence, you create space for others to experience genuine and open communication, relax their own anxieties, and experience the joy of meaningful exchange.

CHAPTER 8:

Engage and Thrive

In the Shambhala tradition, the journey of an individual realizing his or her true nature is illustrated by the analogy of four animals known in Himalayan lore: the tiger, the snow lion, the garuda, and the dragon. The powers of each of these mythic beings represent the gradual unfolding of our natural mind.

The tiger represents the practice of mindfulness in our lives. At this stage we are careful and gentle to ourselves, not bloated by arrogance. Curious about and open to the sounds and messages of our environment, we proceed with discernment, choosing where to step with awareness, inquisitiveness, and confidence and without hesitation, like a tiger in the jungle.

Next is the snow lion, which exudes vibrant energy and cheerfulness. His mindfulness has evolved into joyful discipline, the desire to remain mindful arising naturally as a result of ongoing practice. The snow lion leaps from peak to peak with exuberance and delight because his mind and body are in synch. He is aware, not confused by doubt, and knows what to accept and reject.

The third stage of the journey is symbolized by the mythical bird, the garuda, known as the king of birds. The garuda, which emerges fully grown from its egg and soars into outer space, wings outstretched, represents the fearlessness that comes from facing hope and fear. Having overcome hope and fear, the garuda has tremendous freedom to experience situations with vast vision, and to respond with compassion to the needs of others.

The final stage is represented by the dragon, who controls the natural flow of situations like the seasons and the weather. He abides in the sky in the summer, and hibernates in the ground in the winter. When a storm is needed, the dragon breathes out lightning and thunder.

This analogy is meant to convey unpredictability within the context of predictability. An individual who has arrived at the dragon stage and found his or her true nature appears as wise and stable, but also a bit inscrutable. A person at this level of awareness is energetic and powerful, and has a great sense of humor and playfulness. Stable and relaxed at the same time, the action of the dragon is to create a world of fearlessness, warmth, and genuineness. The activity of the dragon connects vast mind with engaged service to the world.

Inspire and Motivate Action

A person who follows the progression of tiger, lion, garuda, and dragon is someone who is awake in the world and is inspiring others to become their best version of themselves. A person who is in touch with their true nature has the makings of a confident leader. If you're reading this book, you are already a leader of the most important kind. You are demonstrating by your own interest and effort how to be attentive, focused, curious, open, kind, and creative. The ability to lead is based on being able to make a decision, being aware of your own values and also the bigger situation, and then fearlessly taking action. It is a path of going toward the unfamiliar and being willing to be uncomfortable while exercising the freedom to make choices.

As a leader with emotional intelligence, you are tuned into the emotions of others, and are able to empathize with them, give helpful feedback, and inspire loyalty and respect. This helps you further motivate others to work toward shared goals that achieve the needs of your team members and company. If your vision for how to lead includes compassionate action, then you will find and celebrate those who are the helpers on your team. When tapped into your own confidence and open heart, you have tremendous power to inspire others to do their best.

Vail Resorts: Inspiring "Epic Service"

At Vail Resorts in Colorado, the mission is "to create The Experience of a Lifetime for our employees, so they can, in turn, provide exceptional experiences for our guests." The employees take this mission personally, and each year the top fifteen employees are rewarded for outstanding customer service with the Epic Service Award. In the words of one of the employees receiving this award in 2015, there exists in this company an "attitude of loving your job, and wanting to share it with more people is contagious."[73]

"Every day you should learn to see with your heart. I believe that is what Epic Service is," said Mary S., an HR employee and the only employee to win this award more than once. Brian C., an Afton Alps Ski School employee said, "People don't care how much you know until they know how much you care, and we go by that." These employees, and thousands more who are nominated each year, are motivated and inspired by a company that values them and shows it, and by the opportunity to share their own hearts with their customers.

At Vail Resorts, every employee at every level is encouraged to be a leader. The exceptional employee engagement at Vail may be related to the ways in which they develop an emotionally competent core of engaged individuals who work in the midst of a volatile seasonal industry. Vail Resorts' approach to developing leaders is biased toward creating a sophisticated level of emotional intelligence and through a focus on self-awareness, candor and vulnerability.[74] On their website, they share the stories of many of their employees. In the words of Keiran C., Senior Director of Marketing, "The embodiment of our culture is 'Vulnerable Leadership,' with the sense that the more you give of yourself to your team, your peers, your manager, the more you will get back in return."[75]

EKS&H: Attracting Talent Through Love

EKS&H is a nationally recognized accounting and tax firm located in Colorado. You might not expect love to be a key descriptor of a financial services company, but it is in fact what distinguishes this firm from the rest and allows it to compete with the Big Four accounting companies (Deloitte, EY, PwC, and KPMG) in attracting top talent. The employees who choose EKS&H do so because of its exceptional corporate culture built on service, trust, and love.

Lisa Jackson, a consultant at Corporate Culture Pros, detailed EKS&H's inspiring story in a CCP blog post. In the post, she talks about the company's attention and care for their employees and how that reflects the company's key values of customer service, community service, and servant leadership within their company. The company culture page on EKS&H's website opens with the statement, "Focusing on *your* vital interests is our honored obligation." Company CEO Bob Hottman attributes the success of EKS&H to putting their company's purpose and values into action. In Lisa's blog post, Hottman observes, "In an era of constant change, values are what people count on to stay the same."[76] They look for a value match in hiring new employees, and consider those shared values the key factor for the recruit's future success.

They also cultivate a "family culture" in the company. Each floor is divided into four "neighborhoods" that organize fun activities together, such as bowling, ice skating, and happy hours. Partner/manager coaches do the same thing with their individual teams, sharing social time and bonding through fun activities while working hard at the same time.

EKS&H wants to be known as a trusted business advisor, and they live out the values that make it so every day with their focus on their employees, customers, and community. The love and trust the company consciously cultivates inside its walls flows to the outside world, bringing its employees success and the satisfaction of truly being of service.

Love and Joy at Work

The culture of an organization is composed of much more than just cognitive values like being "customer centered"; it is also composed of the *emotional* culture, whether that emotion be fear, resignation, discontent, or jealousy, or the love, inspiration, connection, and joy we have been exploring in this book. Let's look at the positive emotions of love, joy, and kindness and see how they inspire loyalty and satisfaction in both employees and customers.

A Culture of Joy

Vail Resorts' culture embodies not only heart-connection but also joy. Management cultivates joy in their employees, which helps their customers to have fun. It also helps them retain good employees in a competitive industry. Fun is not just for the customers and employees; even management joins in. Their CEO had ice dumped on his head during a recent charity challenge to raise awareness for ALS, and then jumped fully clothed into a swimming pool, followed by 250 other executives and employees. All aspects of the Vail culture support this atmosphere of fun and joy, including handing out pins to any employee seen having spontaneous fun on the job or causing others to have fun. Of course, the positive emotion is contagious, enhancing their customers' experience.

In a March 2016 *Harvard Business Review* article called "Manage Your Emotional Culture," Sigal Barsade and Olivia O'Neill describe a similar work environment at Cisco Finance, where joy is also an explicit cultural value. The authors surveyed employees there, asking them to report on what emotions their colleagues regularly expressed at work, and they discovered that joy was a key driver of employee satisfaction and commitment. In fact, management has even made joy an explicit cultural value, which they call "Pause for Fun." Barsade and O'Neill note how the leaders of the organization support this value in many ways, including making humorous videos that show them pausing for fun.[77]

You can let your creativity and sense of playfulness loose while forming and strengthening important bonds in your workplace by inciting moments of fun. Recently I enjoyed hearing the inspiring keynote speech of Tara Murphy, COO of Achieva Credit Union, the #1 Top Midsize Tampa Bay workplace of 2016.

Murphy shared many stories about what makes Achieva's culture great and the employees so happy. My favorite anecdote was her closing comment about Superhero dress-up days. I laughed as I pictured Cat Woman cashing my check!

Celebrating Love

There are a growing number of companies that list love or caring among their explicit management principles. Some of those companies include PepsiCo, Southwest Airlines, Whole Foods Market, The Container Store, and Zappos. These companies, and others—like EKS&H, described above—celebrate care and compassion in the workplace. The Higher Purpose Statement of Whole Foods, for example, reads: "With great courage, integrity and love—we embrace our responsibility to co-create a world where each of us, our communities, and our planet can flourish. All the while, celebrating the sheer love and joy of food."[78] Being clear about their value on love and commitment to all stakeholders helps Whole Foods to embrace change while staying true to the core of their company.

For those leaders who fear the terms "love" or "compassion," seeing them as too emotional for the workplace, or as "soft skills" that will make them appear weak, I counsel them to consider the power of authentic engagement. When employees, vendors, and clients feel your genuine interest in them, and that you care about their needs and opinions, loyalty is born that cannot be matched by increasing wages or discounting prices alone.

Ultimately, meeting the needs of the customer is the meaning of business, and meeting needs is a definition of compassion. Zappos is another success story that embodies this wisdom. Its mission is "to provide the best customer service possible," and the company says its number one core value is "to deliver WOW through service." On its website, selling shoes is not even listed among the Zappos Family Core Values.[79] I heard Zappos' CEO Tony Hsieh tell a great story that illustrates just how fanatically this service policy is followed by reps attempting to meet the needs of the person calling in to the company. This is the story as I recall it:

After a full day of conferences, Tony and some business colleagues found themselves hungry and in a San Francisco hotel after room service had closed. Tony challenged one of their group to call Zappos customer service in Las Vegas and ask for help. He wasn't joking! He dialed the number and handed over the phone. The caller didn't say anything about being with the CEO of the company; he simply explained to the customer rep where he was and that he was looking for a place that made late-night pizza deliveries. Without missing a beat, the rep said, "Just give me a minute." When he returned to the line he had the numbers of several places that the caller could use to get late-night pizza service in San Francisco. Astonished, the colleague told Tony Hsieh that from that moment on he would always buy his shoes from Zappos.

This kind of service is what makes more than loyal customers—and customers LOVE Zappos! This core customer service value of "delivering WOW" (along with others, like "embrace and drive change" and "create fun and a little weirdness") has driven all of the other policies in the company, and was responsible for leading this start-up online shoe retailer to be valued by Amazon.com for $928 million dollars when it purchased it in 2009. The good news for Zappos fans is that the terms of the merger with Amazon allow Zappos to retain its independent, successful, and inspiring culture of delivering happiness.[80]

If you set an intention to manifest compassionate prosperity, your value for bettering the world through your actions and your desire to manifest profit and financial abundance need not be at odds. By getting clear about your personal and business vision, current values and culture, and desired values and culture, you can delineate a path to achievement that aligns your passion with integrity and care for all with whom you come in contact and influence.

Compassion as a Competitive Advantage

Kindness, in so many ways, is its own reward—but it also pays in profits, brand loyalty, and employee engagement. Remember my Southwest Airlines story in Chapter 6, where the attendant found me a seat on another airline? That act created a loyal customer, and it was encouraged by the compassionate culture of her company.

A few years ago, my husband and I were in New Orleans for a business convention. We were booked into a Ritz Carlton. When we got to the desk, our room was not ready, and we were told we would have to check our bags and wait. The clerk was extremely concerned about that snafu, and offered to upgrade us to a concierge floor. Once we arrived in our room, he had a gift basket and champagne sent up. Not only that, he marked us as customers who should receive that perk every time we visited a Ritz Carlton!

I was so surprised at the time to see how much the clerk cared, but have since discovered that his behavior is not uncommon at Ritz Carlton—a company that identifies their "key success factors" as mystique, employee engagement, customer engagement, product service excellence, community involvement, and financial performance.[81] These are their business priorities. John Timmerman, Ritz-Carlton's vice president of operations, says that financial performance comes last because it's a result of actualizing the other key success factors. Information on everything related to these metrics, from the morale of the restaurant staff in Bali to the number of scuffs on an elevator in London, is collected by the company. If they determine that they are not meeting their key success factors, they figure out what needs to change.

Ritz-Carlton employees are carefully selected and given continuous training and development to ensure they will provide exceptional service to guests. They are trained to detect even the faintest signal of need from a customer. (I was likely annoyed to be delayed in getting into our room, for example, and their actions more than made up for my grievances.) One result of all the attention and development that the employees receive is that the Ritz-Carlton has an employee engagement in the upper 25 percent, and a mere 18 percent turnover—especially impressive considering the industry turnover average for the luxury hotel industry is 141 percent![82] Customer engagement follows employee engagement. A happy employee creates a positive atmosphere that resonates with the customer.

Compassion helps to recruit talented employees, as exemplified by EKS&H. More and more people are looking for purpose and meaning in their work, not just pay, and companies that hold compassion as a core value will attract employees who will thrive and create success in those environments. Compassion also allows for an environment of risk that is necessary for creativity and innovation, as is the case at Pixar. If you are not allowed to fail, you will be afraid to present new ideas. Compassion builds the trust that allows for both success and failure to occur without judgment, and for fresh ideas to be brought to fruition.

Creating a Compassionate Culture

A compassionate culture is one in which people feel cared for and connected, and the voice of each company member is important and respected. Beyond that, success is celebrated, and occasional failure is seen as a learning opportunity. Creative energy flows in this environment, and people thrive. This atmosphere extends to genuine curiosity about how to better connect with customers, suppliers, and community. The compassion expands.

Where is the best place to start to create such a vibrant culture? The simple answer is with the intention and ability to listen well.

A great model for the application of good listening skills is a coaching conversation. Coaching in this context does not refer to a relationship intended to remedy a problem an employee is having but rather an approach to listening well and caring enough to help another person to find their own wisdom. Coaching combines skills and compassionate connection in a way that unifies many of the principles discussed previously in this book.

A culture that embraces coaching and mentoring demonstrates and develops a way of being that allows an organization's people to grow and move from satisfaction to engagement to fulfillment. The skills of a good coach are compassionate mindfulness in action. Developing coaching skills in managers will allow them to transform into leaders who bring out the best in their employees through the care that good coaching communicates. All of the mindful and compassionate practices offered in this book help develop the competencies that a good coach employs.

Nonetheless, explicit training in coaching is really important. Even if it's not in your budget to offer a complete coach certification program, you might consider a daylong or online training in coaching skills for your leadership staff in order to seed this behavior companywide.

Good Coaching is Engaged Mindfulness

The most important skills a good coach exhibits are deep listening, curiosity, and a fundamental trust in human goodness. The manager/coach trusts that the best answer lies within the employee, and it's the coach's role to bring forth that wisdom, not to provide all the answers. This allows for development to unfold, and reinforces the employee's confidence and self-worth.

When you listen to another person in this open-hearted way, understanding, empathy, and even compassion take root. Deep listening taps into the intuition and vast self of the coach and the employee. One of the most difficult hurdles for leaders, and the biggest benefits of practicing coaching with others, is learning to pause and listen—to hold back from jumping in and offering solutions. We have to leave space for and have curiosity about what the other person is thinking, not just fill in the space with what we already know.

In a good coaching conversation, learning flows both ways. As the coach, as you listen deeply to another person, you are simultaneously opening a window into your own beliefs, biases, and desire to share your opinion. Thoughts will arise in your mind when you leave space to listen to your employee, and if you notice but don't act on those impulses, you are deepening your self-awareness and emotional intelligence. When you ask open-ended questions rather than telling the other person what you think, you are demonstrating respect for their ability to contribute to the solution. You are helping them develop self-esteem and self-confidence by showing them that you believe their answers are valuable. Answers that are owned by an employee are also more likely to be acted upon.

It is important in a coaching relationship that you don't get caught in another person's story, drama, or negativity. Instead, you can help them see that there are alternative ways to view whatever setback they may be stuck on, and you can help them develop the skills to see beyond the problems that are restricting their growth. A key is to ask good questions that create learning and promote action. Good questions will lead to greater understanding, as well as a deeper meaning and connection to work. Good questions also generate new ideas. As you model these positive communication skills, you also help your employee to gain insight into how to develop their own awareness and emotional intelligence.

This ongoing coaching approach is developmental for all parties, and may sometimes resemble what is traditionally thought of as mentoring. In some organizations, mentoring is a more formal arrangement between a senior and a more junior individual for the purpose of fostering learning and leadership skills. Both of these approaches—formal mentoring and less formal coaching—can exist simultaneously within a company, and together they express tremendous care for the well-being of the employee.

Let's take a closer look at how EKS&H creates the culture of compassion that attracts and retains their young talent. First of all, they provide a community of support from the start. The first day on the job, new hires are assigned both a buddy—a peer around their own age—to help with social assimilation, and a coach to give them technical guidance and help ensure work/life balance. After the new employee has had a chance to develop their own connections, they are asked to choose a mentor who can guide them to achieve the personal vision they have for their own career. And not only do new employees have coaches, partners have coaches as well. The culture of coaching and mentoring allows all members of the company to bond and make it through the difficult times together.

Coach to Lead

My Barrett Values Center colleague, Tom Rausch, has created a successful program called Coach2Lead that enables the creation of a pervasive coaching culture in companies of every size. He recognized that coaching skills are also leadership skills. He has developed and implemented a rich, blended learning curriculum for creating a compassionate and responsive culture in companies ranging from small consulting firms to the 5,000-person global HR division of Accenture, a leading global professional services company.

A wonderful aspect of this example is the power of one individual with leadership authority and the desire to create a culture of compassion to be able to realize their goal, even with employees from diverse global cultures and at all pay grades. Tim Arnold, the leader of the division at Accenture that undertook this development program, is widely celebrated in the company for his high emotional intelligence, which again demonstrates the importance of this dimension of our personal development. Tim and his leadership team knew Accenture already had a good culture, but they wanted to make it even better so they could maintain their position as an employer of choice in highly competitive talent markets. That's why they agreed to a culture assessment, which led to the implementation of Tom's program.

Before Tom implemented the Coach2Lead program with Accenture, he surveyed the global HR division, spread across seven service centers, to discover where their values lay on the Barrett framework. The assessment confirmed that this division was strong in the foundational values, particularly when it came to systems and performance, and that the leaders of the division had many personal values that reflected a desire for personal transformation and internal cohesion. They wanted to move the company into higher-level values on the Barrett Seven Levels of Consciousness scale, however, and this program allowed them to do that. They were able to move their teamwork from being strong regionally to having whole-system collaboration, from employee engagement to employee fulfillment, and from the leader as a problem solver to the leader as a people developer. The end goal was to create a culture of coaching and recognition that would reach all employees. Within three years, the use of coaching had successfully cascaded across all levels of leadership within the division.

With the foundations of a culture of coaching and recognition in place, Accenture's global HR leadership team decided to improve even more upon their advantages, and they invested in advanced coaching, collaboration, and recognition skills from the top leadership down to the supervisory level. Five years into their journey, they are well on their way to achieving their goal and beyond. They have become a recognized leader in using coaching skills in the workplace and spreading good leadership skills to other divisions within the company. Moreover, frequent and meaningful coaching conversations are now a core tenet of the entire company's (373,000+ people) approach to stimulating performance achievement.

Accenture is recognized as a leader in this approach to performance achievement, and other companies are now emulating their journey. The bottom line is that people are bringing themselves more fully to work as a result of a greater match between their personal values and the values being lived out in their work culture.

Coaching to Develop Trust, Awareness, and Results

Coaching as an ongoing business practice requires some core competencies on the part of the individuals offering this type of support. Attending a coaching training and certification course is the best way to develop confidence in these skills. Meanwhile, it is helpful to understand what is involved in a good coaching experience. What follows is a brief description of how to coach, which I hope will spur you to investigate this practice further. With these competencies, your communication will become more mindful and compassionate.

Practice: Coaching

Step 1: Establish a Space of Mutual Respect and Trust
- Communicate genuine concern (compassion) for employees' welfare and future.
- Establish clear agreements and keep promises.
- Provide ongoing support for new behaviors and actions, including those involving risk-taking and fear of failure.
- Ask permission before coaching in sensitive new areas.

Step 2: Embody Emotional Intelligence
- Stay present for what arises, and be open to not knowing and to taking risks.

- Utilize humor effectively to create lightness and energy.
- Demonstrate confidence in working with strong emotions that arise, and use self-awareness to discern your own feelings from your employees' feelings.

Step 3: Communicate Effectively

- Apply the mindful, active listening skills so critical to allowing someone to feel heard.
- Utilize your ability to focus completely on what is being said.
- Summarize and mirror back what you have heard in order to ensure clarity and understanding.
- Ask powerful questions that challenge assumptions. The best questions are open-ended ones that create greater clarity and move the conversation forward, such as: What have you accomplished since our last meeting? What challenges are you facing right now? What opportunities are available to you right now? What possibilities do you see in that situation?

Step 4: Facilitate Learning and Results

- Help your employee to gain awareness about their fixed ways of seeing situations, allowing for new perspectives and possibilities to emerge.
- Engage the employee in exploring alternative ideas and solutions, and in making new decisions.
- Help establish "stretch goals" that challenge the employee to engage fully in work that is meaningful to them and your department or company.[83]

Meaningful Work, Flow, and Joy

In the workplace, we experience happiness when we feel connected to and receive support from others, and also when we are engaged with meaningful and appropriately challenging work. Work feels meaningful when it is aligned with our core values and purpose, and under the right conditions, performing meaningful work can trigger a state of "flow," a state of peak performance.

The term "flow" was originally coined by Mihaly Csikszentmihalyi, a Hungarian psychologist who has extensively researched this state. Csikszentmihalyi is known as one of the pioneers of the scientific study of happiness, and his most popular book, *Flow: The Psychology of Optimal Experience*, states that happiness is not a fixed state but something that can be developed as we learn to achieve flow in our lives. "The best moments usually occur when a person's body or mind is stretched to its limits in a voluntary effort to accomplish something difficult and worthwhile," he writes. "Optimal experience is thus something we make happen."[84]

If you have ever had a perfect ski day, challenging yourself to master a difficult black diamond run, you have experienced flow as the movement of your body, your response to the moguls, the crunch of the snow, and the swish of your skis just effortlessly coming together. If you have ever engaged in building something, you know the magical feeling of being so totally immersed in what you're doing that the passing of time does not even register. Athletes refer to this feeling as being in the zone, and artists and musicians often describe forgetting themselves or channeling a higher inspiration as they get lost in their work.

The key to flow is absorption in the task you are performing. You are present with it, identified with it. There is a merging of your awareness and the activity you are engaged in. This is not dissimilar to the concept of "non-self" and states of absorption described in Eastern thought theories. We might also describe flow as being immersed in the activity and vast self at the same time. When this happens, we have access to solutions and insights that may be blocked when we are thinking in ordinary ways. Flow is a great driver of innovation, and of joy.

Creating Flow at Work

You can create the conditions for flow to occur at work, and when you do, your actions and decisions will be seamless and you will enjoy intense focus that stays on the task at hand. In the *Harvard Business Review* article "Create a Work Environment That Fosters Flow," Stephen Kotler, author of *The Rise of Superman*, writes, "In a 10-year study conducted by McKinsey, top executives reported being five times more productive in flow. If we could increase the time we spend in flow by 15–20%, overall workplace productivity would almost double."[85] Flow science is in its early research stages, yet is already being applied at Facebook, Google, Toyota, and Patagonia, among other companies.

In a 2016 article for bizjournals.com, Clifford Jones helped make the connection between mindfulness and the breakthrough performance of top coaches and athletes and top performers at work. He noted that the benefits of mindfulness arise from discipline and practice; these are the same requirements for developing any kind of champion. The mindful approach, he says, develops high performance, whether on the basketball court or in the office. Jones provides an interesting example of flow that occurs when—with planning, communication, and accountability—salespeople and customers align: "When your salespeople sell with intention to serve the customer, and your marketing people create more engaging, compelling, relevant stories to attract and convert more customers, you will get better results. You will see and feel the flow."[86] According to Jones, the flow occurs because the business, sales, and marketing leaders share a clear goal and intention, and they are willing to practice and apply mindfulness in the execution of those goals.

The simplest formula for entering this state of non-distraction and enjoyable absorption in your work is to know how to let go of thoughts and reactive emotions. Maintaining a state of calm is the very result of practicing mindfulness, so practicing a few moments of balancing yourself, with focus on your breathing, can provide an opportunity to get present or to reset. If you want to enter a flow state, you start by establishing a sense of calm. Then you make sure that the work you are engaging in has the right degree of challenge. In sports, playing a game against top players might provide this push. At work, the problem you choose to address must have enough challenge to be interesting and engage your skills. Flow happens in the sweet spot where you are challenged enough to be uncomfortable and pushed slightly beyond your skill level, and then feel inspired to meet that challenge. If the challenge is too far beyond your skills, it may induce anxiety, and if it is too easy, you will fall into boredom.

Emotional intelligence comes into play at this point. You need to be able to deal with any distracting emotions that arise. You will need deep focus and undivided attention. Multitasking is out. Shut off all electronic devices, and work in a place where you won't be disturbed. Know your goals clearly so that your focus does not have to wander from the present moment and action. When you find yourself completely immersed in an activity, with your whole being involved and your skills engaged completely, you will be focused, absorbed, and happy. Time flies while you're absorbed in flow!

New Possibilities for You and Work

We live in an amazing time. We now know so much more about the vast potential we have to change our lives by changing our habits, and thereby transforming our own brains. Research into our compassionate nature has shed light on how we've evolved over time and how we can increase our connection to others and our happiness through widening our circle to include those of different backgrounds. We have the possibility to make different choices and become better people. One by one, we can become leaders who create a future informed by a trust in human goodness and respect for all. You can be a change leader, helping to create work cultures free of fear where trust is high, people flourish, and better decisions are made through collaboration. You can be a champion for this transformation in your own workplace.

Start a Meditation Program at Work

Once you have begun to practice mindfulness, you may be inspired to share your discovery with others—or, as you begin to change from the inside out, others may start to notice your enhanced calm, effectiveness, or creativity and ask you to share your secret. Either way, every successful workplace mindfulness program begins with just one or two champions. Last year I personally heard the stories of two such leaders who started small and grew a mindfulness revolution in their companies. The first is Golbie Kamarei, a global program manager at the world's largest asset manager BlackRock, who spoke at the Mindful Leadership conference held in Washington DC in November 2015. The second is Peter Bostelmann, Director of Mindfulness at SAP, who shared his story in 2015 at a gathering of teachers of the

Search Inside Yourself (SIY) model of training mindfulness and emotional intelligence that was developed at Google.

In 2013, after returning from a trip to a yoga ashram where she practiced meditation, Kamarei decided that she wanted to share what she had learned with her coworkers. She knew that in their conservative business environment, she needed to describe the benefits in terms of business principles. When she got back from her trip she explained to her team that what she was offering was a mind training to improve focus and attention. Kamarei said that the performance orientation was important to get people in the room; her hope was that once they began meditating, they would feel the other benefits for themselves.

The first sessions were held in a conference room that Kamarei reserved two times a week for thirty minutes. A memo was sent out to the entire New York office and sixty people showed up; in the weeks that followed, the program spread through word of mouth. As of last year, 1,500 people in seventeen different countries have become part of Kamarei's meditation community, which is now called the BlackRock Meditation Program.

Kamarei stresses that it is important to know your own company culture, and to describe the practice and benefits in a language that makes sense within that environment. Whenever she ran into skepticism while building the BlackRock Meditation Program, she shared quotes from participants to communicate the benefits. These were simple things like, "It makes me more open and receptive to colleagues, and I also leave a meditation session in a much better mood." She also collected hard data on results, because quantifying the impact was important in the BlackRock culture. She sent out a survey to show what a strong impact that the program was having, and the responses revealed that participants were 84 percent better at managing their emotions at work and 91 percent better at managing time and energy.

A staggering 90 percent also reported reduced stress, and 83 percent reported increased focus and decision-making abilities.

Kamarei now sends out a weekly e-mail that reaches all participants in the program, worldwide; the responsibility for keeping the program specific to individuals participating in other offices and regions of the world, however, falls to local volunteers who keep it personal and relevant. Today the BlackRock Meditation program has an executive sponsor and includes discussion of mindful leadership and how it can impact the culture of the company. This program, which started with one person, has grown through the engagement and participation of the volunteers and the employees they are serving.

By Peter Bostelmann's own admission, he was a "lone nut" in San Francisco who loved mindfulness and who wanted to start a mindfulness community at SAP, a global software manufacturer, in 2012. Beginning with that intention, he designed two pilots—one on the West Coast of the US and the other in a European country—that utilized the Search Inside Yourself program. The first pilots had a total of fifty participants over the two locations, and they were very successful. On average, the participants rated their experience as a 6.35 out of 7.

Bostelmann believes that anyone can start a mindfulness program in their company by listening to the needs being expressed by their colleagues, using the business language appropriate to their culture, and talking to everybody they can about their intention, especially people at the top. He recommends "being your own CEO"—just getting out there and starting something, not waiting for permission. Eventually, as the results come in from your pilots, you will learn more and gain support and executive sponsors to accompany your grassroots effort.

In Bostelmann's case persistence paid off. By 2014 he had run eight pilots in two locations, each with 350 attendees, and had established three mindfulness communities in SAP world-wide. Momentum was building and the average ratings for the program were still high, 6.53 out of 7. By this point he was ready to roll out and scale the program through an SAP internal teacher training and a shift from grassroots to an official sponsored global practice. By 2015, Bostelmann held the title of Director of Mindfulness at SAP, and mindfulness communities had been established in eighteen SAP locations. That year, forty-six SIY mindfulness trainings were held in twenty-one locations in fourteen countries, with over 1,600 attendees each, and the program received an average rating of 4.6 out of 5!

Bostelmann credits the qualities of courage, passion, compassion, and persistence for the success of the program. He began surveying the programs for impact across several factors, and a survey he conducted in a 2014 program with over 300 participants revealed the following benefits:

- 89% Improved ability to reduce stress
- 91% Enhanced clarity of mind
- 79% Increased energy levels
- 91% Improved ability to remain calm
- 73% Shifted leadership paradigm
- 85% Increased ability to connect with others

Both of these corporate meditation programs demonstrate that one individual with the drive to make a difference can have enormous impact on the effectiveness, well-being, and leadership skills in their company by introducing mindfulness. You may be the key to that change in your company!

Ideas that Spread Happiness

Here are a few more compassionate ideas that can contribute to your happiness at work, and that of your employees and coworkers:

START THE DAY WITH POSITIVITY. If you are the boss, gather your team at the start of a project and tell each one of them how much you appreciate their skills and how you know they will do amazing work. Remember to appreciate your own abilities and those of your colleagues on a regular basis to ensure a positive start to everyone's day.

PROVIDE ENCOURAGEMENT TO YOUR TEAMMATES OR EMPLOYEES. Not everyone needs encouragement, but almost everyone performs and feels better when they receive it.

UNLEASH THE GENEROSITY OF APPRECIATION IN YOUR WORKPLACE. Appreciation creates a culture of people feeling valued and trusted, and an environment in which people bring their passion to work.

CELEBRATE THE WINS. Make it a point to cheer for and rejoice over a job well done, a contract won, or a client saying that they love your work. Share the celebration and create some excitement. That picks up everyone's mood.

REMEMBER TO SAY "YES." Yes is powerful; it is additive rather than argumentative. The first rule of improv comedy performance is to always say "yes, and," rather than "no" to any line you are given. This allows a situation to flow. In improv, "no" can stop a scene. In any situation, in fact, negation can be a motivation killer. If we remember that rule at work, there will be more momentum, collaboration, and innovation from working together.

FIND TIME FOR PLAY AND FUN. Ten-minute bursts of physical activity can boost workers' mood and performance. UCLA public health professor Toni Yancey's book *Instant Recess* prompted Kaiser Permanente and the Henry Ford Health System to adopt her practice of planned recess breaks at work. Throw a Nerf ball, dance at your desk, run around the office—do whatever you want as long as it's fun, and schedule it a few times a day for maximum benefit.

We spend so much of our lives at work; imagine how great it will be when compassion rather than fear is the dominant emotion. When you are able to uncover your natural power and wisdom through the mindful practices you have learned, you will be more relaxed and productive, and genuinely happier. It all comes down to love. Love what you do, care about your coworkers, have compassion for yourself and for difficult people, meet the needs of your clients, and always do your best. When we operate from our innate human goodness, there is no limit to what is possible. Your open heart turns the key that will enable a future of cooperation, collaboration, openness, and shared prosperity. And that's just what is needed to address our volatile, uncertain, complex, and ambiguous times.

Appendix A:

Table of Exercises and Practices

CHAPTER 7

CHAPTER 8

End Notes

CHAPTER 1

1 Dale Carnegie Training, "Engaged Employees Infographic," http://www.dalecarnegie.com/employee-engagement/engaged-employees-infographic

2 Gallup poll, "Employee Engagement," January 13, 2016, http://www.gallup.com/poll/188144/employee-engagement-stagnant-2015.aspx

3 Victor Lipman, "Why Are So Many Employees Disengaged?" *Forbes,* January 18, 2013, http://www.forbes.com/forbes/welcome/?toURL=http://www.forbes.com/sites/victorlipman/2013/01/18/why-are-so-many-employees-disengaged/&refURL=https://www.google.com/&referrer=https://www.google.com/

4 Amy Scholten, M.P.H, "10 Signs That Your Workplace Is Toxic and What You Should Do About It," *Inner Medicine Publishing,* http://www.innermedpublishing.com/toxic%20workplace.html

5 Jill S. Goldsmith, J.D., LAC, NCC, "Mindful Leadership in a World of Distractions," *Huffington Post,* June 1, 2016, http://www.huffingtonpost.com/jill-s-goldsmith-jd-lac-ncc/mindful-leadership-in-a-w_b_10225152.html

6 Feris Jabr, "Why Your Brain Needs More Downtime," *Scientific American,* October 15, 2013, https://www.scientificamerican.com/article/mental-downtime/

7   Ibid.

8   Emma Seppala, *The Happiness Track: How to Apply the Science of Happiness to Accelerate Your Success,* Harper Collins, 2016

9   Parker Palmer, 2015 Naropa University Commencement Address, "Living from the Inside Out," *Courage & Renewal,* June 9, 2015

10 Shali Wu and Boaz Keysar, The University of Chicago, "The Effect of Culture on Perspective Taking," *Association for Psychological Science* Vol 18 – Number 7, 2007, http://www.news.uchicago.edu/releases/07/pdf/070712.keysar.pdf

11 Dr. Becca Levy, Yale School of Public Health, "The Power of Positive Thinking," *Best Health* Readers Digest, http://www.besthealthmag.ca/best-you/wellness/the-power-of-positive-thinking

12 Alix Spiegel, "Hotel Maids Challenge the Placebo Effect," Heard on Morning Edition, NPR, January 3, 2008, http://www.npr.org/templates/story/story.php?storyId=17792517)

CHAPTER 2

13 Sean Silverthorne, "Shuuuuttt Uppp! Why Your Company Needs 'Quiet Time'," *MoneyWatch*, Feb 23, 2010, http://www.cbsnews.com/news/shuuuuttt-uppp-why-your-company-needs-quiet-time/

14 Ibid.

15 Daniel A. Gross, "This is Your Brain on Silence," *Nautilus,* August 21, 2014, http://nautil.us/issue/16/nothingness/this-is-your-brain-on-silence

16 Ibid.

17 Ibid.

18 Sandy Smith, "Frazzled on the Job: More Than 80 Percent of American Workers Are Stressed Out," *EHS Today,* April 10, 2014, http://ehstoday.com/health/frazzled-job-more-80-percent-american-workers-are-stressed-out

19 Drake Baer, "Why Mindfulness is the Antidote to Multitasking," *Fast Company,* Feb 7, 2014, https://loryros.wordpress.com/2014/02/07/why-mindfulness-is-the-antidote-to-multitasking/

20 Daniel Goleman, "The Focused Leader," *Harvard Business Review* December 2013 issue, https://hbr.org/2013/12/the-focused-leader

21 Britta K. Hölzel, Sara W. Lazar et al, "How Does Mindfulness Meditation Work? Proposing Mechanisms of Action from a Conceptual and Neural Perspective," *Perspectives on Psychological Science,* October 14, 2011, http://pps.sagepub.com/content/6/6/537

22 Ibid.

CHAPTER 3

23 David Gelles, "At Aetna, A C.E.O's Management by Mantra," *The New York Times*, Feb 27 2015, http://www.nytimes.com/2015/03/01/business/at-aetna-a-ceos-management-by-mantra.html?_r=0

24 Melissa Myers, "Improving Military Resilience Through Mindfulness Training," USAMRMC Public Affairs, June 1, 2015, https://www.army.mil/article/149615/Improving_Military_Resilience_through_Mindfulness_Training

25 *Statistic Brain Research Institute, 2016,* http://www.ncbi.nlm.nih.gov/pmc/articles/PMC4471247/

26 Maddalena Boccia, et al., "The Meditative Mind: A Comprehensive Meta-Analysis of MRI Studies," Bio Med Research International, June 4, 2015, http://www.ncbi.nlm.nih.gov/pmc/articles/PMC4471247/

27 Pema Chodron, *When Things Fall Apart: Heart Advice for Difficult Times,* Shambhala, 2000, pp. 1-2

CHAPTER 4

28 Tanushree Mitra and Eric Gilbert, "Have You Heard?: How Gossip Flows Through Workplace Email," Georgia Institute of Technology, http://comp.social.gatech.edu/papers/icwsm12.gossip.mitra.pdf

29 Ibid., pg. 4

30 August Turak, "Steve Jobs and the One Trait All Innovative Leaders Share," *Forbes,* Nov 21, 2011, http://www.forbes.com/sites/augustturak/2011/11/21/steve-jobs-and-the-one-trait-all-innovative-leaders-share/#52703d5e2766

31 Dr. Matthias Gruber, UC Davis, "How Neuroscience Changes the Brain to Enhance Learning," *Neuroscience News.com,* Oct. 2,

2014, http://neurosciencenews.com/curiosity-memory-learning-neuroscience-1388/

32 Ibid.

33 Ibid.

34 Todd Kashdan, "The Power of Curiosity", *Experience Life,* May 2010, https://experiencelife.com/article/the-power-of-curiosity

35 Ibid.

36 SIY Program Video—Daniel Goleman short—"Neuroscience of emotions and decision making," https://www.youtube.com/watch?v=IQX-w87J3Vw

37 Simone Wright, "The 7 Attributes of Intuitive Business Leaders," *Huffington Post,* Sept 17, 2014, http://www.huffingtonpost.com/simone-wright/business-intuition-what-d_b_5833396.html

38 Lauri Nummenmaa et al., "Bodily Maps of Emotions," *CrossMark* Vol. 111 no. 2, http://www.pnas.org/content/111/2/646

39 Malcolm Gladwell, *Blink: The Power of Thinking Without Thinking,* Back Bay Book, Little Brown, 2005

CHAPTER 5

40 Barrett Values Center, free PVA, www.HappierAtWork.com.

41 Dr. Kristen Neff, "The Physiology of Self-Compassion," Self-Compassion website, http://self-compassion.org/the-physiology-of-self-compassion

42 Ibid.

43 Melvin McCloud, "The Ultimate Happiness: An exclusive interview with the Dalai Lama," *Lions' Roar,* July 29, 2016 http://www.lionsroar.com/the-ultimate-happiness-dalai-lama/?utm_source=Lion%27s+Roar+Newsletter&utm_campaign=fd29ce7948-LR_Weekly_Aug_2_20167_29_2016&utm_medium=email&utm_term=0_1988ee44b2-fd29ce7948-21135417&mc_cid=fd29ce7948&mc_eid=5140c573a7

44 Matthieu Ricard, "The Habits of Happiness", TED Talk https://www.ted.com/talks/matthieu_ricard_on_the_habits_of_happiness/transcript?language=en

45 Melissa Dhal, "The Not-So-Secret Secret to Happiness: Be Kinder

to Yourself, Okay?" *New York Magazine,* April 2016, http://nymag.
com/scienceofus/2016/04/the-not-so-secret-secret-to-happiness-be-
kinder-to-yourself-okay.html

46 "Greater Good in Action" website at: http://ggia.berkeley.edu/
#filters=happiness

47 Stephanie Tialka, "How Science Reveals That 'Well-Being' is a Skill,"
Mindful.org, Feb 5, 2016, http://www.mindful.org/science-reveals-well-skill

48 Ibid.

49 Schaefer SM, Morozink Boylan J, van Reekum CM, Lapate RC,
Norris CJ, Ryff CD, et al. (2013) "Purpose in Life Predicts Better
Emotional Recovery from Negative Stimuli," http://journals.plos.org/
plosone/article?id=10.1371/journal.pone.0080329

50 Helen Y. Wang et al., "Compassion Training Alters Altruism and
Neural Responses to Suffering," *Psychological Science,* July 2013 vol.
24 no. 7 1171-1180, http://pss.sagepub.com/content/24/7/1171

51 Barbara Fredrickson et al., "Open Hearts Build Lives: Positive
Emotions, Induced Through Loving-Kindness Meditation, Build
Consequential Personal Resources," *Journal of Personality and
Social Psychology,* Vol 95(5), Nov 2008, 1045-1062. http://dx.doi.
org/10.1037/a0013262

CHAPTER 6

52 Dachner Keltner, "The Compassionate Species," *Greater Good,*
July 31, 2012, http://greatergood.berkeley.edu/article/item/the_
compassionate_species

53 Ibid.

54 Ibid.

55 S.R. Saturn, "Autonomic and Prefrontal Events During Moral
Elevation," *Biological Psycology,* 2015 May;108:51-5. doi: 10.1016/j.
biopsycho.2015.03.004. Epub 2015 Mar 23, http://www.sciencedirect.
com/science/article/pii/S0301051115000629

56 "What About Me?" © 2005 Mipham J. Mukpo. From the CD
Mipham, available from kalapamedia.org <http://kalapamedia.org/>

57 Tenzin Gyatso, 14th Dalai Lama and Howard Cutler, *The Art of
Happiness,* Easton Press, 1998

58   Jean Decety and Claus Lamm, (2006) "Human Empathy Through the Lens of Social Neuroscience, *TheScientificWorldJOURNAL* 6, 1146–1163. DOI 10.1100/tsw.2006.221. http://icpla.edu/wp-content/uploads/2012/10/Decety-Lamm-Human-empathy-through-the-lens-of-social-neuroscience.pdf

59   Chade Meng-Tan, "Compassionate Leaders are Effective Leaders," *Greater Good,* Sept 11, 2012, an excerpt from *Search Inside Yourself.* http://greatergood.berkeley.edu/article/item/compassionate_leaders_are_effective_leaders

60   Chad Meng Tan, *Search Inside Yourself: The Unexpected Path to Achieving Success, Happiness (and World Peace),* Harper Collins 2012

61   Andrea Serino, "I Feel What You Feel if You Are Similar to Me" study, *PLOS,* March 18, 2009, http://journals.plos.org/plosone/article?id=10.1371%2Fjournal.pone.0004930

62   Adam Bryant and David Rock, "A Boss's Challenge: Have Everyone Join the 'In' Group," *New York Times* "Corner Office" interview, March 2013, http://www.nytimes.com/2013/03/24/business/neuroleadership-institutes-chief-on-shared-goals.html

63   Jason Kanov et al., "Compassion in Organizational Life," *American Behavioral Scientist,* Vol 47 no. 6, Feb 2004, http://webuser.bus.umich.edu/janedut/Compassion/Comp%20Organ%20Life.pdf

64   From my personal notes from a 2013 interview from Wisdom 2.0, Jack Kornfield and Bill Ford, https://www.youtube.com/watch?v=bqUkz1dLa_E

65   You can learn more about this training program at: https://www.zingtrain.com

CHAPTER 7

66   You can find an easy link to this guided meditation on the webpage for this book, www.HappierAtWork.com.

67   Travis Bradbury, "Emotional Intelligence Will Supercharge Your Career and Just Might Save Your Life," *Forbes,* March 3, 2016 http://www.forbes.com/sites/travisbradberry/2016/03/03/emotional-intelligence-can-turbocharge-your-career-and-save-your-life/#79eb2b6c5306

68 Ed Catmull, *Creativity Inc.: Overcoming the Unseen Forces that Stand in the Way of True Inspiration,* Random House, April 2014, p.x

69 Ibid., p. xvi

70 Ibid., p.65

71 Ibid., p.86

72 Warren Berger, *New York Times* article, "The Power of Why and What If," *New York Times,* July 2, 2016, http://www.nytimes.com/2016/07/03/jobs/the-power-of-why-and-what-if.html?_r=0

73 You can watch a video of the awards ceremony at: https://www.youtube.com/watch?v=7WrmA1uS-Xw&list=PL1fS_svorUs7A7cHSbeFVXGOm754t0Bpj&index=27

74 Gerald R. Wagoner, PhD., "Vail Resorts, Role Model: Creating Experiences of a Lifetime," Culture ROLE MODELS, July 2016, http://culturerolemodels.com/july-2016.html#vailresorts

75 Vail Resorts website: http://www.vailresortscareers.com/our-culture/leadership-and-development

76 Lisa Jackson, "For Love or Money? Attracting and Growing Top Talent is Key to EKS&H Success," *Corporate Culture Pros* blog, August 9, 2016, https://www.corporateculturepros.com/for-love-or-money-attracting-and-growing-top-talent-is-key-to-eksh-success/

77 Sigal Barsade and Olivia O'Neill, "Manage Your Emotional Culture," *Harvard Business Review,* January-February issue 2016, https://hbr.org/2016/01/manage-your-emotional-culture

78 Whole Foods Market website, The Higher Purpose Statement of Whole Foods: http://www.wholefoodsmarket.com/mission-values/core-values

79 Zappos website, Zappos Family Core Values, http://www.zappos.com/core-values

80 Alistair Barr, " Zappos CEO Distance Shoe Retailers Culture From Amazon," The Wall Street Journal, October 20, 2015, www.wsj.com/articles/zappos-ceo-distances-shoe-retailers-culture-from-amazon-144536734

81 Jennifer Robison, "How the Ritz Carlton Manages the Mystique," *Gallup Business Journal,* December 11, 2008, http://www.gallup.com/businessjournal/112906/how-ritzcarlton-manages-mystique.aspx

82 Ibid.

83   This practice was adapted from the International Coach Federation
     Core Competencies, which you can find on their website at: http://
     coachfederation.org/credential/landing.cfm?ItemNumber=2206

84   Mihaly Csikszentmihalyi, *Flow: The Psychology of Optimal
     Experience,* Harper Perennial Modern Classics, Paperback—July 1,
     2008

85   Stephen Kotler, "Create a Work Environment That Fosters Flow,"
     Harvard Business Review, May 6, 2014, https://hbr.org/2014/05/
     create-a-work-environment-that-fosters-flow

86   Clifford Jones, "What CEOs Can Learn From Top-Performing
     Coaches, Athletes and Entertainers," *bizjournals.com,* September
     20, 2016, http://www.bizjournals.com/bizjournals/how-to/
     growth-strategies/2016/09/ceos-learn-from-top-coaches-athletes-
     entertainers.html

87   Toni Yancy, *Instant Recess,* University of California Press, November
     2010

Acknowledgments

The writing of this book was a labor of love on my part and a labor of patience on the part of others. It included months of piled up papers and books for research and hours of ignoring everything else. I couldn't have done it without the kindness of my wonderful husband, G Van Gils. He has been my support in all ways through the writing of my manuscript. I can't thank him enough for his generous spirit and meticulous proofreading powers. My sons, Alex and Jonathan, have likewise inspired me to persevere in this work, and were kind enough to read early versions of my writing. Family thanks would not be complete without expressing my gratitude to my parents, who have always encouraged me in every way possible.

I truly feel I would not have ended up with the book I envisioned without my incredible editor and She Writes Press publisher Brooke Warner. Brooke is a consummate professional who pushed me to expand, revise, and polish my original writing to her exacting standards. Her personal style felt strong, warm, and supportive all at the same time. I feel so fortunate to have had Brooke helping me to be my best!

I also want to express my appreciation for the encouragement and guidance I received from Jill Cheeks and John Eggen of Mission Marketing Mentors, and Christine Kloser of Get Your Book Done. I want to thank James Clark, co-founder of Room 214, Jim Ruberg, Managing Director of TiER1 Performance Solutions, Tom Rausch, Principle Consultant at TiER1, Gerald Wagner, President of Academy of Culture Ambassadors, and Lisa Jackson, Principal of Corporate Culture Pros for their interest, encouragement and contribution to this manuscript. I am deeply grateful to Katie Andersen who contributed subtle and important edits to this document at the final stages. If I have forgotten anyone, please forgive me and know that I appreciate the wisdom and generosity of all my friends, family and clients that made this book what it is.

The most important influence on my thinking and training that allowed this book to be written are my teachers, Sakyong Mipham, Rinpoche and the late Chogyam Trungpa, Rinpoche. Their wisdom and compassion allowed me to experience the possibilities that are shared in this book.

About the Author

photo © tk

Gayle Van Gils is an author, leadership consultant, and life coach whose approach opens both the minds and hearts of her clients. Her intuitive, direct, and caring process supports greater focus, engagement, and connection, and a productive and compassionate workplace. Gayle's specialty brings together her extensive experience as a mindfulness teacher with the practical solutions and real-life work she has conducted as a business consultant and executive coach. She has an MBA from the Anderson School at UCLA, and is a certified instructor of Search Inside Yourself, the mindfulness and emotional intelligence training developed and proven at Google. She is the founder of the consulting, training, and coaching company Transform Your Culture, and is a senior meditation teacher in the Shambhala Buddhist lineage. Through her teachings both in person and through online courses, Gayle has helped thousands of people to find more peace, energy, inspiration, joy, and success in their lives and businesses.

Gayle and her husband, Gerard, live in St. Petersburg, Florida and have two sons, Alex and Jonathan, who are both musicians. When she is not busy working or practicing meditation, she loves to get her hands dirty in clay and create large sculptural pieces for her home and yard.

To learn more about Gayle or her work, visit www.transform yourculture.com and connect with her on social media:

 facebook.com/GayleVanGilsAuthor

 @gaylevangils

 linkedin.com/in/gayle-van-gils

SELECTED TITLES FROM SHE WRITES PRESS

She Writes Press is an independent publishing company founded to serve women writers everywhere. Visit us at www.shewritespress.com.

Drop In: Lead with Deeper Presence and Courage by Sara Harvey Yao. $14.95, 978-1-63152-161-4. A compelling explanation about why being present is so challenging and how leaders can access clarity, connection, and courage in the midst of their chaotic lives, inside and outside of work.

The Clarity Effect: How Being More Present Can Transform Your Work and Life by Sarah Harvey Yao. $16.95, 978-1-63152-958-0. A practical, strategy-filled guide for stressed professionals looking for clarity, strength, and joy in their work and home lives.

The Thriver's Edge: Seven Keys to Transform the Way You Live, Love, and Lead by Donna Stoneham. $16.95, 978-1-63152-980-1. A "coach in a book" from master executive coach and leadership expert Dr. Donna Stoneham, The Thriver's Edge outlines a practical road map to breaking free of the barriers keeping you from being everything you're capable of being.

People Leadership: 30 Proven Strategies to Ensure Your Team's Success by Gina Folk. $24.95, 978-1-63152-915-3. Longtime manager Gina Folk provides thirty effective ways for any individual managing or supervising others to reignite their team and become a successful—and beloved—people leader.

Think Better. Live Better. 5 Steps to Create the Life You Deserve by Francine Huss. $16.95, 978-1-938314-66-7. With the help of this guide, readers will learn to cultivate more creative thoughts, realign their mindset, and gain a new perspective on life.

The Way of the Mysterial Woman: Upgrading How You Live, Love, and Lead by Suzanne Anderson, MA and Susan Cannon, PhD. $24.95, 978-1-63152-081-5. A revolutionary yet practical road map for upgrading your life, work, and relationships that reveals how your choice to transform is part of an astonishing future trend.